YOU'RE NOT A COUNTRY, AFRICA

YOU'RE NOT A COUNTRY, AFRICA

A Personal History of the African Present

Pius Adesanmi

PENGUIN BOOKS

PENGUIN BOOKS

Published by the Penguin Group
Penguin Books (South Africa) (Pty) Ltd, 24 Sturdee Avenue, Rosebank,
Johannesburg 2196, South Africa
Penguin Group (USA) Inc, 375 Hudson Street, New York, New York 10014, USA
Penguin Group (Canada), 90 Eglinton Avenue East, Suite 700, Toronto,
Ontario, Canada M4P 2Y3 (a division of Pearson Penguin Canada Inc)
Penguin Books Ltd, 80 Strand, London WC2R 0RL, England
Penguin Ireland, 25 St Stephen's Green, Dublin 2, Ireland (a division of
Penguin Books Ltd)
Penguin Group (Australia), 250 Camberwell Road, Camberwell, Victoria 3124,
Australia (a division of Pearson Australia Group Pty Ltd)
Penguin Books India Pvt Ltd, 11 Community Centre, Panchsheel Park, New Delhi
– 110 017, India
Penguin Group (NZ), 67 Apollo Drive, Mairangi Bay, Auckland 1310, New
Zealand (a division of Pearson New Zealand Ltd)

Penguin Books (South Africa) (Pty) Ltd, Registered Offices:
24 Sturdee Avenue, Rosebank, Johannesburg 2196, South Africa

www.penguinbooks.co.za

First published by Penguin Books (South Africa) (Pty) Ltd 2011

ISBN 978-0-14-352754-1

Typeset by Nix Design in 10.5/14 pt Life
Cover designed by mr design
Printed and bound by CTP Printers, Cape Town

MESSAGE FROM CHINUA ACHEBE:

Africa is a huge continent with a diversity of cultures and languages. Africa is not simple – often people want to simplify it, generalise it, stereotype its people, but Africa is very complex. The world is just starting to get to know Africa. The last five hundred years of European contact with Africa produced a body of literature that presented Africa in a very bad light and now the time has come for Africans to tell their own stories.

The Penguin African Writers Series will bring a new energy to the publication of African literature. Penguin Books (South Africa) is committed to publishing both established and new voices from all over the African continent to ensure African stories reach a wider global audience.

This is really what I personally want to see – writers from all over Africa contributing to a definition of themselves, writing ourselves and our stories into history. One of the greatest things literature does is allow us to imagine; to identify with situations and people who live in completely different circumstances, in countries all over the world. Through this series, the creative exploration of those issues and experiences that are unique to the African consciousness will be given a platform, not only throughout Africa, but also to the world beyond its shores.

Storytelling is a creative component of human experience and in order to share our experiences with the world, we as Africans need to recognise the importance of our own stories. By starting the series on the solid foundations laid by the renowned Heinemann African Writers Series, I am honoured to join Penguin in inviting young and upcoming writers to accept the challenge passed down by celebrated African authors of earlier decades and to continue to explore, confront and question the realities of life in Africa through their work; challenging Africa's people to lift her to her rightful place among the nations of the world.

Chinua Achebe

For Alfred and Lois Adesanmi

CONTENTS

PREFACE

What is Africa to me? That is perhaps the most significant question ever asked by one of the continent's diasporic sons, Countee Cullen, in a famous poem titled 'Heritage'. The question of what Africa means has exercised the minds of some of the continent's best thinkers in the twentieth and twenty-first centuries. It stands unanswered at the ideological core of pan-Africanism, Negritude, nationalism, decolonisation, and all the other projects through which Africans have sought to understand and restore their violated humanity.

The essays assembled in this volume represent my attempt to make meaning of rather than answer the question. From narratives covering the last thirty years of my life, to reflections and perspectives on topical African and black diasporic issues, the essays approach the meaning of Africa from the perspective of how that continent has defined me as a member of the human race and a cultural self. I have criss-crossed the continent of Africa as a writer, a scholar of its cultures, and an admirer of its diverse geographies and peoples. I have taken my inevitable identity as African across Europe and the Americas.

The only lesson I have learnt in my travels is that you never get to define Africa. Africa defines you in various contexts and for various people. This enigma that is Africa could very well be the reason why Abioseh Nicol, a poet from Sierra Leone and a member of the anti-colonial nationalist generation of African intellectuals who wrote and published mostly in the 1950s and 1960s, exclaimed in the poem titled 'The Meaning of Africa':

> You are not a country, Africa,
> You are a concept,
> Fashioned in our minds, each to each,
> To hide our separate fears
> To dream our separate dreams.

A concept fashioned in our minds, each to each, to hide our separate fears, to dream our separate dreams. That is the closest to a definition of Africa that I have ever found. That Africa of the mind, which hides our separate fears but also enables our separate dreams, is the Africa you will encounter in these essays. A number of the essays, especially the more political ones in Part Three of the book, were written in reaction to burning issues of the day in Nigeria as they unfolded at the time of writing. I have left the essays in their original shape even where the originally informing contexts have changed or evolved. Some others first germinated as blogs in online ezines before morphing into their final shape in the manuscript. I thank the various blogs and news portals that have provided the platform for trying out my ideas over the years.

Part One of this collection explores how the cultures and traditions of rural Africa gave me an identity in the first ten years of my life in Isanlu, my hometown in Nigeria, and how that identity reacted to contact with and influences from the Western world. The essays in Part Two are thematically united by travel: they present the many meanings of Africa I have encountered on the continent and in the West. Part Three presents my interventions in the perpetually vexatious business of dealing with Africa as represented by Western spokespersons. The final part presents my reflections on numerous issues affecting Nigeria, the continent's most populous country.

PART ONE

ISANLU

1

Oota

Among the two dozen or so names that I was given when I came for the third – and what my parents fervently hoped was the last – time, Dad and Mom finally settled for Adebola Oota Adesanmi. That Yoruba combo survived only the first decade of my life. On my tenth birthday, in 1982, it suddenly occurred to my parents, Alfred and Lois Adesanmi, both ferociously more Catholic than the Pope, that it just wasn't going to cut it for their precious only son to arrive at the Spiritan Catholic seminary in eastern Nigeria with a combination of utterly pagan Yoruba names. Such was their devotion to Roman Catholicism that they were determined to pray and do all that was necessary to have me enrol at the major seminary after high school.[1]

Naturally, all our kinsmen in Isanlu, my parents' hometown in Kogi state in central Nigeria, believed that the Adesanmis were completely crazy. How else to explain their strange desire to sacrifice their only son to Catholic priesthood? The implications were simply too ominous. Wasn't it obvious that as a Catholic priest I wasn't going to have children of my own and

3

continue my father's lineage? I grew up hearing village elders regret that my father went to the UK to study and white people messed up his head. Whoever heard of parents praying for their only son to sign up for a vocation that would signal the end of their family line? In Africa? What was the world coming to?

And so the gift I got for my tenth birthday was the excision of a crucial aspect of my identity and ties to a traditional Yoruba and African world view. My parents dropped my middle name, Oota. That left me as Adebola Adesanmi, but that was still not good enough for their Catholic sensibilities. So they revived Pius, my baptismal name that had never been in use until then, and made it my first name. Adebola, my original first name, was shoved into the middle. Thus, in one fell swoop, the African schoolkid that used to be known as Adebola Oota Adesanmi disappeared and Pius Adebola Adesanmi was born on his tenth birthday.

My family name, Adesanmi, had originally been Ifasanmi, meaning 'I have found favour with Ifa'. The European missionary priests who baptised my grandfather when he was pacified and converted in the early decades of the twentieth century would not tolerate Ifa – a Yoruba 'pagan' deity – in the church. They therefore guillotined the offensive 'Ifa' from my family name and asked for the Yoruba word for crown. '*Ade*? Okay, your new name shall be Adesanmi.' As my family is not royalty, I still believe to this day that those missionaries had only one crown in mind when they renamed my grandfather: the crown in Buckingham Palace. In essence, my family name tells me that an imperialist British crown which I don't give a rat's ass about augurs well for me. For my last name, Adesanmi, literally means 'I have found favour with the crown'! *Named for Queen Victoria*, Chinua Achebe had said of his own Christian name in a famous essay. For some of us, it rings home. Literally.

But Africa has always been known to have funny ways of resisting total erasure by Christianisation, civilisation, modernity, and all the other glittering gifts that came with Europe's civilising mission. Thus, my 'pagan' name, Oota, resisted eradication and clung to my mother's tongue, to be used sparingly only on the occasion of extremely solemn mother–son conversations. 'Oota, Oota, Oota, you are heading out to France. Remember whose son you are. Remember that the Catholic Church is your first family.' The nightclubs and women of Paris ensured that I visited my first family by attending Mass very regularly at the Église Saint-Eustache: at least once or twice every six months. Or: 'Oota, Oota, Oota, what is this we hear that you now drink alcohol? Do you want to kill your parents?' I would reply in the negative and reassure Mom very sincerely that nothing of the sort was happening, while probably caressing the second bottle of Merlot or downing a respectable helping of cognac, wondering what mysteries of African motherhood would make a woman imagine that her full-blooded, hormone-laden, over-six-feet-tall black son in his riotous early twenties could live in the West and avoid booze and (white) girls.

Mom was not the only one who clung to Oota. All the elders in Isanlu alternated between Adebola (which they shortened to Bola) and Oota during my formative years. Like Mom, they called me Oota at their most ponderous and pensive moments, indicating their awareness of the fact that *I am story*. I began to pay serious attention to Oota when I encountered Negritude poetry and philosophy as an undergraduate student of French studies. You do not get into the poetics of Léopold Sédar Senghor, Aimé Césaire, David Diop, Léon-Gontran Damas, and Edouard Maunick without developing a thirst for the finer details of stories of origins and beginnings. You do not study the writings of the Haitian *indigenistes* and remain indifferent to where the rains of culture and history began to beat you as a black African in the world.

When I encountered these new discourses in my first year as an undergraduate, it also happened that the most popular undergraduate course in the neighbouring Department of Religions at the time was a course entitled Esu. Esu is the Yoruba deity who urgently needs to sue Christianity for defamation of character. Christians have ruined his otherwise good name. Unable to find a Yoruba equivalent for the Christian Satan/ Devil, European missionaries reached for the closest equivalent and that is how Esu had the misfortune of entering the Yoruba Bible as Lucifer and his aliases: Satan, the Devil, etc. Today, hundreds of thousands of ignorant Yoruba Christians in Nigeria still go about believing that Esu is Satan or the Devil. The sheer audacity of an undergraduate course entitled Esu made many of us audit that course.

The courses I took on Esu and Negritude heightened my thirst for roots and sources. I now needed to know why I was named Oota. So one day during long vacation (we call it 'long vac' in Nigeria – the equivalent of summer in the West) I asked Mom about it. Oota is the Yoruba word for stool. No, not that stool! I mean the wooden stool that is commonplace in West Africa. My mother would certainly not have named me after the messy end product of the call of nature. When my father returned from England to start his career in the first decade of Nigeria's independence, a job, a house, and a car were waiting for him. Next thing on the agenda: make babies. Two girls came in quick succession and stayed. For a long time, nothing happened. My mother began to panic: the eternal damnation of women in my part of Africa was setting in. Mom had no male child.

Anxiety. Stress. Tension. Whenever my father's people greeted my mother in the streets of our village, the ordinary hello took on inflections that only an African woman 'cursed' with solely female children would understand. Village men whose spinster daughters had gone to teachers' training college or were doing Grade II certificate courses began to pay nocturnal calls on my dad. Those visits made Mom extremely edgy and uncomfortable. There could be only one reason why men with marriageable daughters would visit at night a man whose wife couldn't bear him a male child. Then Mom had a boy! But after one look at this ugly world, the little creature decided instantly that things were much better where he came from and returned there. Two years later, Mom had another boy. Same scenario: he died within one month, like the first boy. Mom was definitely on her way to becoming Dad's senior wife ...

Then I came – the third boy in a row! The villagers had absolutely no doubt that I was the same troublesome male child who had come twice previously. Even Dad and Mom temporarily dropped England, modernity, and Catholicism and truly believed that it was my third coming. The Yoruba *abiku* belief system – an *abiku* is a roaming spirit-child fated to repeated crossings between the worlds of the living and the dead – brushed aside all their acquired Western-ness. There is no educated/Westernised/Christianised African who doesn't know when to temporarily (and quietly) suspend the Western influences around us and let Africa take over the process of making meaning in our lives. The facade of the West returns only when we have solved a particular problem *the African way*. Even Senghor hid his belief in totems from the arrogance of the proud races.

As the story of my being an *abiku* child gained legitimacy in the village, my paternal grandmother was not going to let me fool everybody again. She promptly branded my face. This explains why my undergraduate students in North America can't have enough of me whenever I teach J.P. Clark's or Wole Soyinka's 'Abiku', two poems that have made the *abiku* narrative globally famous. Very few colleagues enjoy the extraordinary privilege of being able to stand in front of an undergraduate class and tell them that those two poems are remarkably accurate accounts of his or her life. That they are not just superstition. Those poems are indeed my biography. I came for one and the repeated time, to borrow the second line of Soyinka's poem.

I survived the first month. The second. The third. The fourth. Like Ezinma's mother in *Things Fall Apart*, my mom began to dare to hope that I had come to stay. The nocturnal visits to offer my dad a second wife came to an end. Mom was greeted normally again by my father's people. After the fifth month, Mom concluded that I had indeed decided to stay. So she named me Oota, *the symbolic stool on which she was finally able to sit securely in her husband's house.* She now had a proper seat in her husband's house and among her husband's people. She was no longer what the Yoruba call *fidihe* – sitting tentatively on one buttock! Naturally, my two elder sisters – one a lawyer, the other a nurse – hate that name. They don't like it when Mom calls me Oota. I don't blame them. It certainly cannot feel too good for them to think that the two of them combined were not sufficient to be the Oota that could secure my mother's place in her husband's house. So, they tend to dismiss that name as superstitious African nonsense.

Not so my mom and all the elderly members of my very large extended family for whom that name is at once memory and story. In Africa, a single name is often one family's encyclopaedia. That is why to this day the village elders are ever so pensive when they call me Oota. Some tease me by asking if I know the stories and memories my mother packed into that one name. They grin in satisfaction when I tell them the story as I heard it from my mom, adding a bit here, correcting a detail there. 'Ah, son, I was there when it all happened. Your mother really tried. You wicked boy. Did you have to treat her like that? Did you have to come twice before making up your mind to stay?'

My dad passed in 2007 but my paternal grandmother is still alive and kicking. We call her Mama Isanlu, and she is the first person I go to see as soon as I arrive in the village on my regular summer trips home from North America. After all these years, Mama Isanlu still doesn't completely trust her *abiku* grandson.

You get a sense that she feels she cannot afford to sleep with both eyes closed as far as my case is concerned, lest I pull a fast one on everybody and return to the great beyond as is the wont of my ilk. So, I undergo intense interrogation while she is mixing concoctions – 'How long are you staying this time, son?' The length of my stay will determine the nature of the concoctions I would drink, eat, mix with my bath water; the incisions that would go on my head; etc.

I let her do all that. I endure all the incisions, drink all the concoctions because I no longer believe that those things are pagan or idolatrous practices as I was taught in Catechism years ago. Outside, my furious Catholic mom, who won't go near those things Grandma is doing to and with her son, is waiting impatiently for us to go to evening Mass. I indulge my mom too and accompany her to Mass, wondering if Jesus and the Holy Ghost will take kindly to the invasion of their space by all the ancestral spirits and forces Grandma has only just injected into my corporeal being. It is the same old Roman Catholic church building in the village, where Grandpa Ifasanmi had become Adesanmi. Now his grandson returns to the same church as Oota, his body reeking of concoctions that are supposed to be manifestations of African spirits and ancestors, wondering in his scholarly mind if Africa isn't exacting a little revenge on the West ...

2

DON WILLIAMS: FRAGMENTS OF MEMORY

America invaded my formative years in Nigeria through culture, mainly books and music. Indian (Amitabh Bachchan!) and Chinese (Bruce Lee!) films relegated American (John Wayne) movies to a distant background. In high school (Titcombe College), James Hadley Chase was our most mesmerising path to America. The irony of preferring the America of an enthralling British author was supremely lost on us. We did not just read Hadley Chase, we *lived* each title and its captivating characters. You boasted to schoolmates that the trouble was finding which Chase you hadn't read. Confessing to not having read a particular Hadley Chase title was a felony. I learnt the hard way when I owned up to not having read *Want to Stay Alive?* back in Form Two. 'Ah, you mean you don't know Poke Toholo?' my friends asked in horror, their tone acquiring an instant whiff of superiority.

Poke Toholo is the dreaded American Indian who goes about killing rich law-abiding white people in the novel. Postcolonial theory was to come years later and ruin my happy ignorance by making me take a second hard look at Hadley Chase's representation of blacks and Native Americans in his novels. Trust postcolonial theory to spoil the fun! Anyway, none of the hordes of 'serious' American writers – black, white, or Native American – I would later read ever came close to Hadley Chase in giving me that unique adrenalin version of America. Nobody writes America like Chase. Today, you may raid my personal library and make away with John Dos Passos, Ernest Hemingway, Bernard Malamud, John Steinbeck, Russell Banks, Sherman Alexie, Philip Roth, Jodi Picoult, and Toni Morrison. Just don't touch my Hadley Chase collection! Bernard Madoff, Robert Stanford, and other postmodern American fraudsters came a couple of decades too late. They would have provided fantastic material for a Hadley Chase thriller on America. Imagine Madoff married to Helga Rolfe!

We escaped the enchanting world of Hadley Chase's America only to be 'arrested' by American musicians. Now this is where it gets really interesting. Of all the genres of American music that formed part of our cultural consciousness as young Nigerian schoolkids, country music came to acquire a significance that, years later, I would be at pains to explain to my American friends, especially African Americans. Kenny Rogers entered Nigerian ears mainly with 'The Gambler'. Dolly Parton's 'Coat of Many Colors' resonated with us because so many of us could relate to the lyrics. Nigerian musicians like The Mandators even recorded a reggae version of the song. I doubt if they ever got permission from Dolly Parton to release her song in Nigeria. After all, you just went ahead and recorded your own version of any American song in the African postcolony.

Before he found Christ through the miracles of prosperity Pentecostalism that is now invading Africa like a swarm of locusts, Pastor Kris Okotie did a fantastic version of James Taylor's 'Carolina in My Mind'. And there were songs by

11

Johnny Cash, Waylon Jennings, Emmylou Harris, The Judds, and Ronnie Milsap, whose 'Daydreams About Night Things' signalled the beginning of restless adolescent explorations of forbidden warrens of pleasure with the opposite sex that would end up in the ears of white Catholic priests at confession.

Then there was Don Williams! How a country musician from Floydada, Texas, became one of America's greatest gifts to the ears of my generation – pre-teen schoolkids in faraway Nigeria – is a matter that should detain all students of Africa and transnational aesthetic crossings. Perhaps it was that voice? That voice! That deep hickory baritone that comes only once in a generation! For Don Williams's voice is to country music – no, to music – what Zinedine Zidane's feet were to the art of football in his heyday. Halfway through high school, we had already become mobile libraries of Don Williams's songs. We did a lot of things to our vocal chords in the vain hope of approximating the malty and textured baritone of the master in 'You're My Best Friend'. Helen Reddy's 'Best Friend' comes close in melodiousness, especially the version she did while playing a nun in the film *Airport 1975*, but it is not Don Williams. And if it ain't Don Williams, it ain't Don Williams. And nothing did it for us like waking up in the morning to 'Lord, I Hope This Day is Good' playing on the radio!

Each song had its practical, contextual uses. Whenever you were mad at your friends, you whistled 'Fairweather Friends' in their hearing in class; when you were down and needed inspiration, 'If Hollywood Don't Need You' was your best bet. For reunions, nothing did it like 'It's Good to See You'. And the love songs! No one does love songs like Don Williams. Pure poetry. The very best. And we went to work, pilfering lines and verses from so many of the songs for use in the little love letters we wrote to the girls we fancied. Most Nigerians of a certain age would remember those secondary school 'love missives' that started by asking the girl if she was 'in a good condition of health, if so, doxology'! 'Listen to the Radio', 'I've Got a Winner in You', 'Senorita', 'Lay Down Beside Me', and many other Don Williams love songs found their way into our love notes. If, God forbid, the girl snubbed you outright, you sang 'She Never Knew Me' loudly within earshot. For a one-night stand gone bad after 'social night' – a night of libertine proclivities which we were granted every last Saturday of the month – you sang 'Rake and Ramblin' Man', making sure she heard the part that said 'do I look like a daddy to you?' To win your girl back after a break-up, nothing worked like lines stolen from 'If I Needed You', the Townes Van Zandt song that Don Williams did in a fantastic duet with Emmylou Harris.

Then it happened. When we were somewhere between 100 and 200 Level at the university, a devastating urban legend began to make the rounds: 'Have you heard the news? Don Williams is a racist!' Don Williams a racist? We were crushed. In our young minds, it was simply unthinkable that our hero could be a hater of black people. You see, country music came to us in Nigeria without the baggage of America's race demons. Who among us was going to be the first to declare that he no longer liked those fantastic songs? That would have been as felonious as renouncing James Hadley Chase. Years later, as I taught Zola Maseko's celebrated film *A Drink in the Passage* in a graduate seminar at Pennsylvania State University, it was easy for me to get into the perplexed sentiments of those South African white racists in the film who admired the genius of an art work produced by a black man in an apartheid context that predisposed them to deny the existence of any such thing as a black genius.

How do you love the art and hate its creator on account of his or her colour? How do you admit that a work of art by a black artist is pure genius while believing that black people have no genius? A curious version of that central problematic of Zola Maseko's film had confronted us in the urban legend of Don Williams's alleged racism. How do you love the songs of a country artist who hated your race and who you were now supposed to detest in return? Somehow, Don Williams was luckier with us than Joseph Conrad was with Chinua Achebe. He survived that terrible urban legend. Suspicion of racism wasn't enough to dampen our enthusiasm for his music.

Then I went to America after completing my doctoral studies in Vancouver, British Columbia. As I packed, the Nigerian friends who frequented my apartment in those last Vancouver days made away with my Don Williams CDs. After all, I was going to America, the ancestral seat of country music: the home of Don Williams. It was only natural to expect that I would have my fill of Don Williams in America. No need to carry coals to Newcastle, right? Wrong! The first shock Americans give the Nigerian is that they know nothing about country music! Let me explain. Country music for the contemporary American is Tim McGraw, Brad Paisley, Kenny Chesney, Faith Hill, Alan Jackson, Carrie Underwood, Martina McBride, Reba McEntire, George Strait, and a few Canadian sprinkles. Americans who are really into country music may know a thing or two about older generations of country artists. But rare is that American who has ever heard of Don Williams! And in the reckoning of many Nigerians of my generation, if you don't know Don Williams, you don't know country music. Period!

Country music and Don Williams became sites of contested cultural discoveries and encounters between my new American hosts and me. I still recall those occasions when friends would call to welcome the new African faculty member and discover, to their pleasant surprise, that I was 'into country music'! Moreover, I wasn't just collecting CDs and following the Grand Ole Opry closely; I also had a respectable library of books on the history of country music as well as biographies and autobiographies of notable country artists. My own pleasant surprise was always about how little they knew about country music. And there was the inevitable heartbreak they gave me: when they knew country music at all, they'd never heard of Don Williams. Some rubbed salt on my wound: 'You mean Hank Williams?' Then came the torrent of questions: Country music in Africa? Who would have thought of that? And I would think how odd it was that Don Williams enjoyed in Nigeria the superstardom denied him at home. Friends from Ghana, Zambia, and Tanzania would later confirm that Don Williams was not the exclusive property of Nigerians. They also grew up listening to the master. This only added to the amazement of our American friends.

By far the most delicate situations came with my African American friends. What the heck was this African brotha doing? What's with him and the music of southern white racists? That was pretty much the situation the first time I hosted some African American graduate students who had graduated and were leaving town. They couldn't get over my investment in country music. Not even the evidence of my no less passionate investment in jazz, rap, and R & B helped. The fact that my collection of the musical masters of the Harlem Renaissance was almost complete made matters worse. One of them wondered aloud, albeit jokingly, how I could defile the masters by stacking country music trash so close to them in my collection. I even dared to put Dolly Parton on top of Satchmo (Louis Armstrong) in my CD rack!

He was sure that such an arrangement of CDs could give the Reverend Al Sharpton a heart attack. I was sure that he would be even more scandalised if he heard the much more suggestive and evocative translation of his sentence – putting Dolly Parton on top of Louis Armstrong – in my language, Yoruba: *Dolly Parton wa loke Satchmo*! Only one of them had heard of Charley Pride, one of country music's greatest masters, an inductee of the Grand Ole Opry and the Country Music Hall of Fame, who happens to be an African American like them. I told them that we also listened to Charley Pride 'when we was young 'n' growin' up in Nigeria', trying out my dysfunctional Ebonics. I told them jokingly but truthfully that my humanism was expansive enough to accommodate Satchmo, Salawa Abeni, Mozart, Ladysmith Black Mambazo, Ajadi Ilorin, Rossini, Comfort Omoge, Kassav, Lady Gaga, Beethoven, Rihanna, Obesere, and most certainly Don Williams!

Today, as I look at the American musical scene from Canada, I wonder what those African American friends of mine would make of the fact that the hottest name in country music at the moment is as black as they are. I'm referring, of course, to Darius Rucker, whose last two albums have been chart busters, what with hits like 'Don't Think I Don't Think About It' and 'It Won't Be Like This for Long'. For me, the thing about Darius Rucker is not that he is an African American singer rocking country music at the moment. It's just that his voice is the closest anybody has ever come to Don Williams, my Don Williams!

3

DEWDROPS OF MEMORY:
ISANLU AND THE ISLAM
OF MY CHILDHOOD

Today, the rest of the world associates Nigerian Islam with the murderous Islamism of Al-Qaeda and the Taliban. For good reason. Since 1980, Islamic fundamentalists have turned the northern part of Nigeria into an annual theatre of blood. It was not always this way. While I was growing up in Isanlu, Islam was always present and I came to know that religion intimately. The Islam that I knew was already in full swing decades before my head kissed the earth of Isanlu. As is the case all over Nigeria and Africa, life in Isanlu was suffused in colourful forms of traditional spiritual expression until Christianity arrived in the early twentieth century and things began to fall apart.

Of the scores of Isanlu rituals and traditional festivals my maternal grandfather told me about as a kid, I met only the Ogun, Sango, Egungun, new yam, and a handful of other festivals, and they were all in intensive care at the hospital because of life-threatening injuries sustained from contact with

Christianity. I still have vague recollections of the severance of the neck of that propitiatory Ogun dog[2] and the subsequent procession through the town by Ogun adherents whom my outraged Catholic parents dismissed as idol worshippers and pagans. Sadly, Ogun and Sango festivals did not make it. They perished in Isanlu somewhere in my teenage years. Somehow, I still think Ogun and Sango were lucky to have died peacefully in the hands of orthodox Christianity like Catholicism and ECWA (Evangelical Churches of West Africa). Imagine what manner of undignifying death Pentecostalism – which came later – would have visited on them.

To survive, Egungun masquerades and new yam festivals had to devise ways of dealing with Christianity, the impertinent mosquito that elected permanent residence on their scrotum. Egungun had to 'de-spiritualise' or 'de-paganise' itself and become an annual Isanlu Day cultural festival in order to be left in peace by Christians. Today, the annual Egungun festival in Isanlu has zero connection with spirits and ancestors. It is just a secular aesthetic ceremony meant to entertain people (one month before Easter!) and to tease the camera lenses of curious European and American visitors. I have only just launched a private initiative to find, buy, and save some of the Egungun masks before they are destroyed by Enoch Adeboye's[3] Pentecostal soldiers in Isanlu. Or before an enterprising European or American beats me to it! I don't want my two-year-old daughter to have to pay to see Isanlu Egungun masks in a European or American museum in the future. That is why I still cannot visit African collections in museums in Paris and London. I cannot pay to see my own stolen property.

In my hometown the new yam festival took more radical steps to survive the onslaught of Christianity: it simply passed (like African Americans 'passing') and became a Christian ritual! I wonder why scholars of Africa have devoted scant attention to this interesting phenomenon of an ancestral ritual passing. The new yam festival became part of the annual harvest and thanksgiving activities on the calendar of every Christian denomination in Isanlu, especially my local parish of the Catholic Church. In fact, I knew it exclusively as a Christian rite until I became a serious student of my culture and history. In Isanlu, you took the first and choicest yam harvest from your farm to the Christian altar. (Chinua Achebe's readers should bear in mind where the people took their yams to after the fall of Ezeulu. That is why Achebe's works are more than fiction for some of us.) In essence, no one of my generation in Isanlu and other parts of Yagba land has any memory of the new yam festival as a traditional ritual. For my generation, it is an important feature of the Christian calendar!

In essence, the people of Isanlu are predominantly Christians whose grandparents and great-grandparents followed the familiar script of encounter with European missionarisation. I would put Isanlu's population at ninety-five per cent Christian. The regular denominations held sway – the Catholics, Anglicans, Methodists, and ECWA. There were also the Africanised white-garment Aladura denominations. The hurricane of Pentecostalism would breeze in ferociously only in the 1980s. I have yet to study how Islam crept into this almost seamless shift from Yoruba spiritualities to Christianity in Isanlu, but my hometown has always had an indigenous Muslim minority, located mostly in the Bagido/Mopo axis of the town.

By the late 1970s, itinerant Fulani herdsmen, who used to guide their cattle annually through our farmlands – causing significant damage to crops but allowing us to feast on delicacies like *kilishi*, *wara*, *fura*, and *nono* – requested land on which to settle. Our king and his council of traditional chiefs deliberated and actually gave them land and space close to the king's palace. Thus was born in the early 1980s the part of Isanlu we now call Sabon Gari, or Sabo for short, with its typical Hausa-Fulani *suya* market layout. The influx of Hausa-Fulani settlers swelled the pre-existing indigenous Muslim population of Isanlu. The children and grandchildren of these settlers now speak mostly Yagba dialect and Yoruba.

The Isanlu of my formative years was thus an interesting theatre of non-violent coexistence between dominant Christianity, minority Islam, and the precarious remains of traditional Yoruba spiritualities. The relationship between Christianity and Islam in Isanlu was even more interesting. Virtually every Christian denomination as well as the Muslims founded a primary and secondary school in the town. For instance, the Catholics owned the local cottage hospital, two primary schools, and Saint Kizito's College. My father reigned supreme as principal of Saint Kizito's in the 1970s before he was transferred to head Saint Augustine's College in Kabba in 1978. The Muslim community in Isanlu owned Ansar-Ud-Deen (we called it Ansaru) Primary School and Oluyori Muslim Comprehensive High School. Unforgettably, my first teenage exploratory kiss with my first true love took place in the corridors of Ansaru.

For some reason I need to study seriously now that I am assessing Isanlu history closely, none of these educational institutions discriminated in their admission policy. Parents enrolled their children freely in any school of their choice without religious considerations. Thus, the Catholic primary schools had lots of ECWA, Anglican, and Muslim pupils. Ansaru probably had more Christian than Muslim students, given Isanlu's dense Christian population. Christian teachers taught at Ansaru; Muslim teachers taught at the Christian schools. The ECWA mother of my first true love was once headmistress at Ansaru. My best friend, a Pentecostal, attended Oluyori Muslim High School.

These constant flows between faiths did not stop at the level of educational institutions. The faiths worked out unwritten codes of collaboration and mutual co-presence by sharing one another's celebrations. I remember our annual Catholic thanksgiving in September. Donation time and our catechist, Mr Alegbemi, would mount the rostrum and make a roll-call of every Christian denomination in Isanlu. Each delegation – Baptist, Anglican, Methodist, ECWA, CAC (Christ Apostolic Church), etc. – would rise up when announced and dance to the altar with their envelope to the accompaniment of inspirational choruses by the host choir and a generous shower of holy water by the officiating priest, with yours truly as altar boy holding the water bowl. The last on Mr Alegbemi's list were always representatives from the Isanlu mosque. The Muslim delegation would also approach the altar with their envelope. The following week, it was the turn of another Christian denomination and the scenario that played out the previous week at the Catholic church would be repeated. Thus, from September through November of every year, the entire Isanlu community moved from one church to another, celebrating the host church's annual harvest and thanksgiving festival. And these celebrations always included a delegation from the mosque. Dewdrops of memory ...

The celebrations rolled into Christmas and New Year festivities which the Muslim community also celebrated with us. On Christmas Day, after Mass, my mother would dish out the rice and chicken and load the steaming plates on trays that we the children had to carry to designated partakers of her Christmas largesse. I still recall my resentment and bitterness that, after my father had been served, the choicest parts of the chicken went to the white Catholic priests at the mission. I would grumble all the way to church with that tray of rice and chicken meant for the Reverend Fathers Léo Leblanc and Gérard Fournier on my head.[4] I had more reason to be unhappy if Bishop Alexius Makozi (now Bishop of Port Harcourt Diocese) happened to be around. That meant a definitive death sentence for two cocks that I had been told belonged to me and that I had fed conscientiously throughout the year – I would be lucky if I got the intestines, legs, and necks of the unfortunate fowls! My cousins and nephews carried similar trays of food that my mother had dished out for an alhaji here, an alhaja there, and other members of the Isanlu Muslim community. Dewdrops of memory ...

The Muslims too had their celebrations and festivals that involved the Isanlu Christian community. My favourite was the return from pilgrimage by any Isanlu Muslim who had been privileged to go to Mecca. What a feast! We the children, Christians and Muslims alike, would form a long procession through the town with the new alhaji or alhaja, singing and dancing:

> *Barika re oh eh*
> *Barika re oh ah*
> *Alhaji to re Mecca to bo*
> *Barika re*

> Congratulations
> To the faithful
> Who went to Mecca
> And is back among us

The procession ended at the new alhaji's or alhaja's house with eating, drinking (not alcohol o!), and merriment. We Christians joined in Islamic choruses offering thanks and praise to Allah for the safe return from Mecca of that Isanlu son or daughter. In fact, the entire Isanlu community celebrated every Muslim festival. Between inter-denominational and inter-religious festivities and trans-religious educational institutions, growing up the way I did in Isanlu meant encountering Islam as a member of the family even though no member of my immediate or extended family was a Muslim. Dewdrops of memory ...

There were, of course, minor tensions. The occasional flash of anger when, as children playing football after classes, a Christian mocked the faith of the Muslims as *imo lile* (difficult religion) – a contraction of which is the popular Yoruba cognomen for Islam, *imole*. That was the most serious denigration of Islam that I knew growing up. To put the impertinent Christian kid in his place, we would join our offended Muslim playmates in singing:

> E ye pe Musulumi loni mole
> Elesin Isilamu ki se mole
> Elesin alafia ki se mole
> Eni ba pe Musulumi l'oni mole
> Ko kewu ri, ko bere
> A lai mo kan ni

> Call not the Muslim
> An adherent of a difficult faith
> A religion of peace it is
> If you have never prayed, never inquired
> Yet label the Muslim faithful
> You are just ignorant

Some of these boyhood quarrels ultimately ended at home with parents on all sides enjoining all parties to respect one another's faiths and to remember that we were all *omo Isanlu*.

Boyhood passed, young adulthood came. Location: University of Ilorin mini-campus. My undergraduate years came before the era of sanguinary campus cultism in Nigeria. Apart from our studies, all we knew were the excitement of *aluta*, police tear gas, and the menace of campus Pentecostal fellowships. Campus born-again Scripture Union Christians could never be content to assemble for fellowship in one or two large groups in consideration of other members of the campus community.

Rather, following the bad example of the public nuisance value of their parent organisations on the Lagos–Ibadan Expressway,[5] scores of little subgroups answering to every name from Tabernacle to Maranatha, from Deeper Life to Rhema, from Redeem to Mountain of Fire via Living Faith and Christ Embassy would take over every available lecture room, the one trying to out-scream the other as they spoke in tongues and invited the Lord's fire on powers, principalities, dominions, and other enemies all night long. A group of five fellowshipping students could take over a hundred-seater lecture room, screaming in tongues through the night. This made the campus very hostile for those of us who needed to study to pass exams. Those wailing all night were already assured of the Pentecostal miracle of passing without studying. Dewdrops of memory ...

The Islam I met as an undergraduate at this Pentecostalism-infested mini-campus of the University of Ilorin was not the caliphal Islam of the town of Ilorin proper. I remember it now only as an Islam of early morning feasting and celebration during the Islamic fasting season. That was a season of early morning largesse and abundance that my friends and I, all Christians, looked forward to! The fasting Muslim students had to wake up every morning to break their fast. They called it *sari* in their local Islamic parlance. I guess there is something in their religion that enjoined them to share that meal happily with their friends and neighbours, irrespective of religious differences. We waited for the call of their muezzin, who would yell in the hostel corridors every morning, 'Wake up! Wake up! It's time for *sari*!' We the Christians would be the first to wake up and start the rounds from room to room, inviting ourselves to the meals of Muslim students! You only need to remember the financial precariousness of university life to appreciate the importance of this *awoof* (free) Muslim breakfast that I never missed in my four years of undergraduate study. Dewdrops of memory ...

The Islam I encountered from Isanlu to Ilorin in my formative years was not just about *awoof* food and festivities. That Islam also fed my mind and expanded my world. My father despised a mind that didn't devour books daily, and he never stopped buying books and expanding his vast personal library until he died in 2007. I tearfully recall now the hours I had to spend reading in his company in that library – with a rap on the head if I forgot what he told me the day before about the Almoravids or the Hamitic hypothesis – while regretting the five-a-side football game of 'set' I was missing with my friends, hoping he would let me go before the end of the game and spare me the exaggerated accounts of my friends at school the following day. '*Ah, Pius, game ana yen gbona*! Very hot game! You missed o!' Dewdrops of memory …

When my father died, that expansive library became my most precious inheritance. Dad was a trained historian, with a BA and an MA in African history. He was halfway into a PhD in African history at the Ahmadu Bello University, focusing on the trans-Saharan trade, when his health failed him and he abandoned the programme in the mid-1980s. He never really recovered from that illness. Because he was in that university's tradition of African history, his library contained impressive materials on Islam in West Africa, especially the Islamic scholarship that emanated from Timbuktu. He subscribed to *Tarikh*, collected material on Islamic poetry and philosophy. My fascination with the travels and writings of Ibn Battuta started in my father's library at home. That was where I also encountered names like Rumi, Ibn Khaldun, and Al-Maghili. Dewdrops of memory …

This is the Islam I knew. This is the Islam that fed my belly and my mind. Now, I watch in horror, in stark contemplation of a faith gone awry. How did this Islam arrive at the conclusion that it was okay to sever the head of Gideon Akaluka, mount it on a spike, and chant *Allahu Akbar* triumphantly in the streets of Kano? What about Christianah Oluwasesin, clobbered to death in the name of this Islam by high school boys? Why have the educated elite from this part of Nigeria pretended thus far that they can do nothing about this nonsense for which they all, without exception, must be held responsible? Have they given a thought to forming alliances and embarking on sensitisation campaigns to wrest Islam from the control of a deadly and opportunistic political elite? We must ask the question, what is this Islam which is not Islam?

4

PROFESSING DANGEROUSLY: AN AFRICAN PROFESSORIATE IN THE EYES OF A COUNTRY BOY

Back in secondary school, one of my close cousins, Bola Akanbi, fell in love with university professors. Bola and I were then sharing the same bedroom in my mother's staff quarters bungalow in the sprawling compound of Titcombe College in Egbe. Bola's father, one of those colonial, missionary-trained, no-nonsense secondary school principals like my own dad, was doing his doctorate at the University of Ibadan.

Dr Samuel Akanbi and my father belonged to a generation of Spartan educationists who spiced their impeccable Queen's grammar with Latin and sported a district officer 'parting' (a straight line carved through the hair with a comb) on the right or left side of their heads. They could drive you home at the end of a school day to cane you in front of your parents, who thanked them generously for it before your father proceeded to give you a supplementary caning for the disgrace. Infrequently, Bola earned a hop-along trip when his dad was going for consultation with his doctoral supervisor at Ibadan. Those were the days.

That was before the academic haemorrhage to Euro-America that Paul Tiyambe Zeleza has analysed so brilliantly in a number of works. Many of the big names in the faculties of arts, education, and the social sciences were still around in Ibadan. That's where and how Bola's love of professors began. Bumping into some of those names must have done things to the impressionable mind of a secondary school kid. Bola would return to Titcombe from Ibadan to regale us with stories of Professor this and Professor that, laced with routine schoolkid exaggerations and a considerable swagger of superiority.

Before long, Bola's fascination extended beyond the University of Ibadan and he came to acquire an encyclopaedic knowledge of the names of professors from most of Nigeria's universities. His hobby was to reel out names of professors, stressing every syllable and looking at us as if we were baboons when we professed ignorance of those names. 'You mean you don't know Pro-ffe-sssor Jacob Festus Ade Ajayi? What about Pro-ffe-sssor Obaro Ikime? Pro-ffe-sssor Eskor Toyo? You don't know them either? *Suegbe l'eyin boys wonyi o.'* And Bola would strut away like a royal peacock, hissing and bemoaning the fate that placed him in the company of such ignorant peers as us. In essence, if you were a professor in the 1980s in any Nigerian university and you were worth knowing, Bola knew you in his little corner of the world at Titcombe College.

Then the radio announcements came in dizzying succession in the 1980s: 'I, Colonel Joshua Dogonyaro of the Nigerian Armed Forces' (1983); 'I, Colonel Joshua Dogonyaro of the Nigerian Armed Forces' (1985). 'I, Brigadier this; I, General that'. We had coups and counter-coups. Mine gradually became a generation that knew more about martial music broadcast on early morning national radio than we knew about any other aspect of Nigerian national life. The national ethos was changing. All the values we knew were being bastardised by the military before our very eyes. Principals like my dad or Bola's dad had to watch out. You had better be able to recite the national anthem or pledge 'with immediate effect' or a considerably younger Group Captain Salaudeen Adebola Latinwo, military governor of Kwara state, could barge into your office through the window – always through the window – and 'frog jump' you. On national TV, we saw those despised soldiers publicly frog jumping Nigerians of our fathers' generation, and then slapping and horsewhipping them in the street. In graver situations, the soldiers could deny you your share of 'essential commodity' (essenco).[6]

These changing scenarios were playing out as we approached 100 Level. During our transition from secondary school to university, Bola's diction had changed. Now that's a paradox. Here was a schoolkid who spent his time in secondary school memorising the names of a mind-boggling number of Nigerian professors. This same kid got to the university and army generals became his new fascination. His encyclopaedic mind dropped the database of professors and seamlessly replaced it with a brand new database of generals. He was now also less enthusiastic about university education. He was only just there at the university – going through the motions. His mind was really on the Nigerian Defence Academy in Kaduna and he spent a couple of years trying to get in. Like most Nigerians of my generation, Bola was seeing possibilities of himself as a newly commissioned military officer first serving as ADC to a military governor before participating in a coup to become a governor himself. In my own moments of messy privacy in the toilet, I would practise at the top of my voice: 'Fellow Nigerians, I, Major General Pius Adesanmi, of the Nigerian Armed Forces ...' That sounded kinda cool.

There is, however, a lot more to why professors crashed from their Olympian pedestal and eventually disappeared from the mind of Bola Akanbi. If we admit that there is a story here that we may now tentatively entitle 'The Rise and Fall of the Nigerian Professoriate in the Mind of One Nigerian Schoolkid', if we also agree that Professors Ayodele Awojobi[7] and Charles Soludo[8] are at antipodal ends of this story, we need to begin to critically map and understand the trajectory that took us from Awojobi's brightness to Soludo's penumbra. We need to know when, where, and how the rain began to beat Nigeria's professoriate, especially in view of an uncomfortable history of dangerous and unethical demissions that Charles Soludo has inadvertently but tragically come to symbolise.

Daniel Elombah, the prolific publisher of elombah.com, has recently offered an excellent dissection of Professor Soludo's ethical about-turns and moral somersaults. What needs to be added to Elombah's treatise is the fact that there are broader national contexts and histories that have led us to Charles Soludo. It is a national malaise, not a regional or Anambra problem. Those contexts and histories are, in turn, linked to what Obi Nwakanma, a prominent Nigerian poet and public intellectual, likes to characterise as the collapse of the 'university idea' in Nigeria. Whereas most analyses reduce the crisis in our universities to empirical and material details – collapse of infrastructure, outdated libraries and laboratories, etc. – Nwakanma has always contended that we have in fact lost the idea behind the derelict structures. The fortunes or misfortunes of the professoriate in our recent history are a good place to start discussing the loss of the university idea.

For what Bola Akanbi had latched onto back in our secondary school days in the village wasn't just the title of professor or the considerable body of knowledge that the wearer of that title is normally deemed to have acquired. That schoolkid plugged into an overarching halo, aura, and awe that devolved from the considerable socio-political, moral, and ethical capital that the Nigerian professoriate had come to acquire in the public space largely due to the critical interventionism and public activism of a long line of engagé professors symbolised by the likes of Ayodele Awojobi, Wole Soyinka, Pius Okigbo, Eskor Toyo, Omafume Onoge, Bala Usman, Adebayo Williams, and Attahiru Jega, just to mention those few randomly. Add to this the collective public profile of the hot literary lefties of a certain era – Professors Biodun Jeyifo, Niyi Osundare, Femi Osofisan and others. Such critical and activist modes of inhabiting the public sphere were what created a certain national idea of the professor-as-demiurge or the professor-as-vates – the image and idea that mesmerised a secondary school kid.

By moving beyond the cocoon of academia and making Africanist knowledge production an expression of the people's will and desire, in the people's language, and always in opposition to the organised banditry otherwise known as the Nigerian state, these engagé professors carved a Gramscian trajectory that came to define the public face of the Nigerian professoriate. You will recall that the Italian Antonio Gramsci, by far one of the most famous thinkers of the twentieth century, gave us the idea of the 'organic intellectual'. In addition to analysing social life according to systemic and scientific protocols, the organic intellectual harmonises and expresses the consciousness and feelings of the people. In this academic professor, town and gown meet and a social vision/mission is born and pursued, often at great personal cost.

It is often wrongly assumed that Ibrahim Babangida, the military despot who ruled Nigeria from 1985 to 1993, destroyed education by deliberately underfunding the universities, wrecking academic and non-academic unions, and triggering a mass exodus of the professoriate by making the words 'professor' and 'poverty' much more than a matter of poetic alliteration. Those are mere empirical consequences of a much more symbolic and graver assault on meaning. Babangida was far too sophisticated a buffoon to be content with merely undoing the professor materially. He targeted the aura and the halo, demoted the demiurge, and vanquished the vates. What Babangida undermined and put on life support were the idea and the ideal that society had vested in the professoriate. General Sani Abacha only needed to remove the oxygen later.

Babangida's strategy was brilliant. Part of the professoriate's capital with the Nigerian public was the idea that an indissoluble union of character and learning inhered in it. Babangida would have none of that Siamese twin. He performed a surgical operation, severed character from learning, and threw the former into a septic tank. To demystify the professoriate, Babangida manufactured two professor types and unleashed them on the Nigerian public: Professor Errand Boy and Professor House Nigga.

Professor Errand Boy was the man Babangida somehow convinced to leave campus and come on board on 'national assignment'. He gave this professor sufficient perks and resources to discourage any idea of a return to campuses he was simultaneously starving of funds. But the real intention was to make the professor's public image pedestrian. That was achieved by bouncing him from post to post and office to office like a ping-pong ball. Chairman of some special agency or parastatal today, minister of some ministry outside of his zone of competence tomorrow, ambassador to some backyard country next tomorrow, back to chairman next week. Professor Errand Boy would, of course, be inherited by subsequent regimes and administrations, and be bounced around by others just like he was by his inventor, Babangida.

The bouncing back and forth had consequences: in the public's mind, the boundaries between professor and office messenger got dangerously blurry. One would almost need a calculator to tabulate the posts held under the military by Professor Jerry Gana alone. The more aura, halo, and social capital the academics brought to the table, the better for

Babangida. Hence he also got Professors Tunji Olagunju, Adele Jinadu, Sam Oyovbaire, and a host of other distinguished academics to constitute an unimpeachable pool of knowledge producers in Aso Rock.[9] And they ran errands with unalloyed love for the military puppeteers. Those who today make grandiose claims about the 'legacies' of the professor-servicers of Babangida forget too easily that whatever the said professors did in terms of bringing so much intellectual firepower and ideas to the governance of Nigeria at the time was subsumed within the symbolic economy of Babangida's subterranean politics: demystify the professoriate. With Professor Errand Boy, the awe was gone. The rash of quota professors being manufactured in the northern part of the country did not help matters in terms of public respect for the professoriate.

From the standpoint of the soldiers, Professor House Nigga was an improvement on Professor Errand Boy. Here, we cross the threshold of errand running into the territory of faith. Professor House Nigga's work for Babangida was not just an assignment he mistook for service to the nation. He saw his job as a sacerdotal mission because he was a true believer who was genuinely in love with his master. Like the house nigga in American lore, if Babangida was sick, Professor House Nigga declared to the nation: 'We are sick'. If Massa Babangida went to France to treat his radiculopathy, Professor House Nigga wore sackcloth, poured ash on his own head, prayed, and fasted till Massa returned. This pathological love of Massa has been known to subsist long after Massa has left office.

Consider this scenario: More than a decade after Babangida left office, you are ill to the point of death in a Boston hospital. This man, whom you served so faithfully at the risk of your own professorial reputation, does not lift a finger to help. Yet you remain a believer, constantly trying to smuggle the tyrant into a nice corner of Nigerian history in broad daylight. Then Babangida's wife lands in a California clinic and you are the first to release an online statement urging prayers for her. What greater love hath a man for his Massa? We are effectively in the province of what Wole Soyinka calls 'inhuman' love when discussing Senghor's infinite capacity to forgive the colonial atrocities of France and still find a *wuruwuru* way to place France on the right hand of the Father 'among the white nations'. This love for Babangida by a professor he somehow convinced to believe that a research centre could forge democratic ethos under jackboots and a pile of decrees is inhuman – inhuman because 'superhuman', according to Soyinka. Are we surprised that our subject is still online today celebrating his role as one of the 'founding fathers' of Nigeria's current constitution – a flawed, illegitimate document imposed on the nation by a bunch of arrogant generals who dared to utter the solemn words 'we the people'?

In Professors Errand Boy and House Nigga, Ibrahim Babangida demystified and pedestrianised the Nigerian professoriate. This was a sophisticated way of preparing the ground for the gaggle of professor-servicers that Sani Abacha would instrumentalise later in his own, much cruder fashion. What Abacha added to Babangida's template was his ability to convince so many credible and impeccable professors that it was possible to work for and with a killer like him and somehow come out of it all with the squeaky-clean reputation with which most of them went in.

The combined effect of Babangida's and Abacha's assault on the professoriate was to erase the halo, aura, and ideal that society had invested in those persons. Ironically, lowered ratings and expectations by society meant freedom to descend even lower, in the logic of 'he that is down needs fear no fall'. This explains a new phenomenon that emerged with the advent of 'democracy' in 1999. I was still in graduate school at the University of British Columbia. I would phone Nigeria and ask casually after Professor X or Professor Y. I got an answer that became increasingly frequent and worrisome: 'Ah, Prof has left o. He has gone back to his local government to contest for chairmanship o. Prof is now a PDP [Peoples Democratic Party][10] chieftain in his local government area.'

The problem wasn't that profs were leaving in droves to join politics. I believe that our tragedy as an African nation devolves from the fact that the best among us have abandoned leadership and governance to the selfish hawks among us. The problem was the kind of politics the professors joined and the terms of engagement – electoral politics as defined and determined by the PDP, by far one of the most corrupt and oppressive institutions ever to bestride the African continent. This is no place to rehash the sorry, disgraceful, and embarrassing profile of that bastard of a political party. Suffice it to say that unrivalled ability to lie and loot and a one hundred per cent deficit in integrity are the party's two most important membership requirements. When Wole Soyinka described Abacha's regime as 'the open sore of a continent',[11] he was describing a counterfeit or 'bend down' open sore. The Peoples Democratic Party in Nigeria is the genuine or original open sore of the African continent.

This purulent political institution benefited immensely from the demystification of the professoriate by the military. With the road to demystification smoothly paved by the soldiers, all the PDP needed to do was to create a worse personage than Professors Errand Boy and House Nigga. Enter the PDP's Professor Nutin Spoil. Where Professor Nutin Spoil is not a regular jobber like Professors Errand Boy and House Nigga before him, he is neck-deep into everything that makes the ordinary people of Nigeria sick and tired of the accursed democracy that has held them hostage since 1999. As electoral umpire, Professor Nutin Spoil is otherwise known as Maurice Iwu; as participant in and beneficiary of the PDP's culture of electoral violence, massive rigging, and daylight political robbery, his name is Oserheimen Osunbor.

This, in essence, has been our compulsory rite of passage to the unfolding tragedy that is Professor Charles Soludo, Nigeria's latest and, according to Daniel Elombah, palpably most disappointing Professor Nutin Spoil. Suddenly we are dealing with the familiar and the strange united for better and for worse in the same body. There is the Charles Soludo that we know: one of Africa's most brilliant economists. A stellar academic trajectory saw him become one of the youngest full professors of economics ever to emerge from Nigeria. Then there is the Charles Soludo that we don't know: he is appointed governor of Nigeria's Central Bank and becomes an overnight billionaire; buys up choice properties in London; sends his kids to private schools in London that only the offspring of Middle East oil sheikhs should be able to afford; joins PDP politics; gets himself an offshore godfather in a dubious character like Chief Tony Anenih; participates in the subversion of democratic ethos within the PDP to emerge as the party's governorship candidate in the forthcoming Anambra elections; roams the land now in a convoy of thugs and with loads of money that he is distributing to buy the election.

Where is the professor of economics? Where is the economics he taught as a professor at the University of Nigeria? Even in secondary school economics, when we read those famous textbooks authored by O. Teriba and O.A. Lawal, one got at least the vague impression that economics is all about the prudent management of scarce resources. Would the students Professor Soludo trained – especially the doctoral students he supervised – be able to square up his gargantuan profligacy with the theories he taught them? What did he teach those students about looting and plundering the resources of the state in Africa? Did he attend graduation ceremonies in his years on campus? Did he wear an academic gown? Did he mouth the usual platitudes about 'character and learning' as the graduands filed past the academic staff? What does he think of all these things now as he spends his loot in the attempt to buy the office of governor of Anambra state? How does he plan to recoup that investment? What's in it for Chief Tony Anenih, his offshore godfather from Edo state? How does the professor feel about bringing himself so low that a charlatan and a buffoon like Chris Uba now feels sufficiently enamoured to ask Nigerians to determine who the criminal is between himself and Charles Soludo? The horror! The horror!

Questions. Questions. Questions. Yet Professor Soludo just happens to be the most famous Professor Nutin Spoil around. Others abound in the system, contributing a restless run of nails to the coffin of what they once professed. Not long ago, some professors in the senate of the University of Benin, led by Professor E.P. Kubeyinje, acting vice chancellor of the university at the time, put their heads together and somehow concluded that it was a great idea to invite Elder Chief Stakeholder James Ibori to deliver the university's 2009 Founder's Day Lecture! A thoroughly embarrassed Nigerian cybercommunity has sufficiently addressed this unbelievable violence inflicted on the very idea of the university by the professors in Benin.

Here are some facts that the specific Professors Nutin Spoil responsible for the invitation knew about James Ibori: (1) he was convicted twice in London in the 1990s for theft and shoplifting; (2) he is wanted in London for money laundering and other related charges; (3) he is still standing trial in Nigeria for corruption. None of these facts discouraged these professors in Benin from giving this convicted felon a university pedestal to address graduating students. The Nigerian people need to know which professors, apart from Professor Kubeyinje, actually sat down in a lecture hall to listen to James Ibori. Hopefully, they had the decency to at least leave their academic gowns at home!

When next our folks in Benin want to invite a guest lecturer, let them borrow a leaf from Obafemi Awolowo University. OAU has just reduced the shame the University of Benin brought on us all – 'us' is the Nigerian academic community – when it recently invited the globally acclaimed human rights lawyer Femi Falana to deliver its Distinguished Alumni Lecture. Let the professors in Benin not tell us that they can find no better alumnus of Uniben than a third-class graduate of that institution convicted twice for theft by the Queen of England. If James Ibori wants to invest some of his huge loot in education as part of a broader process of restitution, there are ways to do it.

Yet Nigerian professors abound, at home and abroad, who are doing this thing the way it ought to be done: quietly, diligently, and steadfastly. From Toyin Falola to Eghosa Osaghae, from Jimi Adesina to Aduke Adebayo, from Demola Dasylva to Obioma Nnaemeka, from Dele Layiwola to Onookome Okome, and thousands like them, Nigerian academe remains the root and home of so many bright stars in the firmament of global academe. But, in the nature of things, the good apples don't get to define the public face of the professoriate. The political jobbers do. Sadly.

PART TWO

DETOURS

5

WE, THE COLONISED!

In August 1998, I arrived in Vancouver from France to begin a doctoral programme in francophone African literatures in the French department of the University of British Columbia. The first week of the new session was devoted to the usual fare of course registration, teaching assistant orientations, and departmental cocktail parties. In all that frenzy, I was able to sense that I had been inserted into a politicised terrain marked by tension between an Anglo-Canadian bloc and a Québecois bloc. I was given an office in a spatial zone dominated by Québecois graduate students in the department. That signalled for me the beginning of what was to be a year-long engagement with Québecois linguistic and cultural nationalism in its most radical ramifications. I expected a lot of new things in Canada. Encountering a ferocious nationalism that tried to appropriate my own identity and history as an African was not one of them!

Those among us who got teaching assistantships to help fund our studies were assigned two to an office. On my second day in our new office, my office partner walked in and introduced himself as a fellow graduate student. After the initial exchange of pleasantries, he asked me the routine questions Westerners often ask about Africa. At one point he said: 'So, you are working on francophone African literatures. Are there any other writers from that region, apart from Senghor and Césaire?' I replied, 'Well, Césaire is not from francophone Africa. That leaves the whole of francophone Africa with only one writer, right?' Missing my sarcasm, he tried another angle: 'What are the challenges for you, an African, working on African literatures?' I didn't exactly know how to respond, so I ventured what I figured was the most sensible answer: 'Roughly the same challenges you could expect to face as a Canadian working on Canadian literatures.'

It was an unfortunate response. I had struck a dangerously raw identity nerve. I had yet to learn that it is a bad idea to label a Québecois ultranationalist, impatiently waiting for the next secessionist referendum, a Canadian. 'Hey, I am a Québecois working on Québecois literature,' my office partner said. 'As someone from a continent that was once colonised by European oppressors, you should know better than to toy with the identity of a fellow oppressed.' He left the office before I had an opportunity to reply, leaving me in utter amazement. *A fellow oppressed?* I couldn't possibly have heard him right. The next morning he apologised for his behaviour, and we got off to a fresh start.

As I reflected on the fact that he had described me as 'a fellow oppressed' the previous day, I asked for clarification. He expressed genuine surprise that the 'very obvious fact' that *we* shared a 'common experience of oppression' at the hands of English colonisers could be lost on me. Then followed a meticulous historical inventory of the 'horrors' of colonial oppression the Québecois have suffered under their Anglo-Canadian oppressors: the ever-present threat of extinction of their language, the economic exploitation of the province of

Québec by the centre in Ottawa, and the 'sickening' reality of a people of French extraction being, technically, subjects of the Queen of England. His every sentence was, of course, generously laced with the phrase *nous les colonisés* – we the colonised!

We the colonised? This phrase, which he used repeatedly during the charged office debates we subsequently had throughout the 1998–99 academic year, would radically unsettle the ideas of Africa's colonial victimhood that I brought to North America. The entire universe of meanings Africa had given to me until then was suddenly threatened by his ideological self-fashioning. For sure, I had read Albert Memmi before relocating to Canada. However, it was one thing to read a Tunisian thinker analysing Québec in the registers of colonial discourse analysis, and another thing entirely to sit a few inches away from someone I considered to be a privileged white man and listen to him unite Africa and Québec as co-victims of the West and white Europeans! For the first time I realised that I had always had a mental conception of 'the colonised' as a clearly defined racial 'territory' within meant for Africans and other people of colour. I never imagined I would one day encounter a white man laying such emotional claim to that territory.

My instinct as an African intellectual faced with this unexpected situation was to go on the defensive, to establish a perimeter around the very zone of oppression to which the white male before me was staking a vehement claim. The type of oppression he was talking about evoked concrete historical and geo-spatial verities that I felt he couldn't possibly grasp. What did he know about oppression? What could evocation of the colonial massacres at Thiaroye, Dimbokro, and Sharpeville mean to him? Did his claims not constitute a second symbolic shedding of the blood of Patrice Lumumba and Steve Biko?

I felt instinctively that if he must gain admission into that conceptual space of colonial violence at all, I could only let him in as the oppressor. It was too much to ask me to share the space of colonialism – to inhabit the 'we' in his 'we the colonised' – with a Western white male, and I made that clear to him. His answer left me breathless. The privileged Western white male was also his problem, his 'colonial master'. He, like me, had been shaped by the anti-imperialist, cultural, political, and nationalist discourses of Québec to envision strategies of resistance against this English-speaking, cigar-puffing, white male in Ottawa who controls his destiny. In fact, his intellectual energies aimed at resisting this English-speaking white coloniser of French Canadians. In essence, *we* were not only united by a common colonial experience, *we* also faced essentially the same enemy – English-speaking whites!

In subsequent discussions, he attempted to convince me, via an Orwellian permutation, that as an African I was even more equal than him in the territory of the oppressed. First, Africa was 'lucky' because the colour line was clearly drawn between oppressor and oppressed. The oppressor did not enjoy the privilege of anonymity. It was not possible to confuse the Boer and the Zulu. Québec lacks that strategic advantage, since oppressor and oppressed are of the same colour, making colonial oppression far less visible than it had been in Africa. Second, because I was born after 1960, I never really knew colonialism as a concrete reality. It was 'only' part of my history and heritage. For him, 'concrete colonialism' was a continuous nightmare from which he may never have the opportunity of awaking, to paraphrase Joyce's famous formulation. Consequently, on the scale of oppression and suffering in the hands of the Western white male, he had greater authentic claims than I, an African!

I subsequently audited courses in Québecois literature and thought, focusing on texts of cultural and political nationalism. I read André d'Allemagne's *Le colonialisme au Québec*, a cross between Frantz Fanon's *The Wretched of the Earth*, Walter Rodney's *How Europe Underdeveloped Africa*, and Aimé Césaire's *Discours sur le colonialisme*. While still refusing to validate his claim to 'my African territory of colonial oppression' and my 'ownership' of the emotions associated with that identity, I began to see where my Québecois friend was coming from. In d'Allemagne's vitriolic prose, Québec bears an incredible resemblance to Kenya, Rhodesia, and South Africa under white settlerist plunder and dispossession. English-speaking Canadians resemble the colonialist ogres and predators in Ayi Kwei Armah's *Two Thousand Seasons*. An unproblematised reading of *Le colonialisme au Québec* would create the somewhat 'dangerous' impression that countries like Ghana and Nigeria were, indeed, more equal than Québec in the territory of colonialist rape.

I also studied the corpus known as *les romans de la terre* (literally, 'novels of the land') in Québecois literature and was amazed by the similarities between the treatment of land in that literary current and the handling of African land in the works of African writers like Chinua Achebe, Ngugi wa Thiong'o, Sembène Ousmane, and Ayi Kwei Armah. Ringuet's novel *Trente Arpents* is the major text of *les romans de la terre*. Reading that novel increased my unease that a white settlerist population was offering me painfully familiar narratives of oppression and dispossession that I was being asked to validate as a fellow colonised. It was impossible for me to close my eyes to the overwhelming structural and thematic similarities between *Trente Arpents* and Achebe's *Things Fall Apart*. The former reads very much like a Québecois predecessor of the latter. I almost committed the heresy of wondering if Achebe had read that novel before writing *Things Fall Apart*. I had that nagging sense of familiarity of plot that never leaves any reader of Sembène Ousmane's *God's Bits of Wood* who is familiar with Zola's *Germinal*.

Ringuet's hero, Euchariste Moisan, and his rural, agrarian clansmen are faced with the implacable advance of 'Western' modernity and cultural imposition represented by the enemies, *les Anglais d'Ottawa* and their 'big brothers' – the Americans south of the border. Inevitably, Ottawa and the United States succeed in placing a knife on the things that hold Moisan and his people together, and they fall apart, to paraphrase Obierika's famous statement in *Things Fall Apart*. Like Okonkwo, Achebe's hero, Moisan ends up in exile in the United States, from where news of the erosion of the cultures and traditions of his native Québec filters to him.

Years have passed since these events occurred in Vancouver, but the spectre of my office partner's conscriptive statement – we the colonised – still looms over my attempts to understand the nature and behaviour of contemporary cultural discourses and politics from the perspective of Africa. I have consistently had to critically reassess my instinctive delegitimation of my Québecois friend's right to stage his own peculiar form of oppression and, more importantly, my refusal to be conscripted into his imagined community of the colonised. On reflection, my handling of that situation speaks to a phenomenon I want to refer to as the territorialising psychology of the oppressed in Africa.

In the nature of things, forms of historical oppression are often racialised and made to behave like spatial territories owned by specific racial-cultural groups. Such emotions eventually crystallise into a people's sensitive heritage. For instance, the transatlantic slave trade as a form of oppression immediately evokes blackness (race), the slave coasts of Africa, the American South, and the Caribbean plantations (space and territory). The colonial 'pacifications' that occurred in Cholula, Soweto, Sharpeville, Thiaroye, and Dimbokro equally have automatic connotations of race, space, and territory. The writer Paul Gilroy makes this point succinctly when he asserts that in situations of 'routine experiences of oppression, repression and abuse', culture 'becomes akin to a form of property attached to the history and traditions of a particular group and regulated by anyone who dares to speak in its name'.

Gilroy argues further that 'the emphasis on culture as a form of property to be owned rather than lived characterises the anxieties of the moment'. When particularly traumatising forms of historical oppression constitute the foundation of a given culture, territories emerge, rooted in the psyche and the collective imaginary of the oppressed, and this process generates the sort of cultural exceptionalisms that have led to the shedding of so much African blood.

Before zeroing in on Africa, let us make some detours. Consider one of the most famous narratives of oppression that we frequently refer to, at least since Sartre, as the 'Jewish question'. For much of their history, the Jews have had to contend with a world that has always insisted on their being either a 'question' or a 'problem', a world that has allowed them only one bloody temporal march from Pharaoh's straw fields to Hitler's crematoria via a traumatic experience of dispersal. It is therefore not surprising that the dual constructs of 'Jewish suffering' and 'Jewish persecution' have become foundational to most articulations of modern Jewish identity in the thought and discourses of various Jewish intellectuals.

Persecution and suffering become psychic, sacrosanct spaces whose 'territorial integrity' must be maintained so as not to 'let in' those who cannot really understand the particularity, the exceptionality of 'our' situation. When oppression is territorialised and made foundational to an exceptional identity, it is capable of generating its own processes of othering and exclusion, as we see in some of the essays collected in the edited volume *The Other in Jewish Thought and History*. Narratives such as Elie Wiesel's *Night* and *The Jews of Silence* function within an implicit ideological paradigm of the exceptionalism of Jewish suffering.

In 'My People', the last part of a volume of essays titled *Out of*

My Later Years, Albert Einstein reflects on the travails of Jewry. While he makes the occasional reference to Palestinian and Arab suffering, there is no mistaking the same streak of Jewish exceptionalism in the 'territory' of suffering that undergirds the thought of the other cited intellectuals. When oppression is transformed into a sacrosanct territory, the implacable spectre of Orwell emerges in which a people's oppression is perceived as being more equal than all other forms of oppression. When a people derives its sense of history, memory, and identity from such an exceptionalist formulation, the articulation of other forms of oppression competing for narrative space is felt as either a threat, an invasion of a sacrosanct territory, or a mockery of one's specific, unequalled historical particularity.

This is the dilemma Edward Said faced as he tried to clear a narrative space for Palestinian suffering within Euro-American landscapes of oppression monopolised by narratives of Jewish suffering and persecution on the one hand, and the Napoleon-is-always-right posture of the American state vis-à-vis the state of Israel on the other. Given this context, how do you narrate Palestinian suffering without appearing to water down the dominant Jewish narrative of suffering? How can one hold the Israeli state responsible for the massacre of Palestinian women and children in Jenin without encountering hostile counter-narratives brandishing Auschwitz as a more politically correct site of suffering? How can one even talk about Jewish historical suffering being transformed into an exceptionalist territory without appearing to be an anti-Semite?

The Nobel laureates Wole Soyinka and José Saramago and the internationally acclaimed South African writer Breyten Breytenbach had a particularly traumatising experience with Jewish exceptionalism and its grip on the West. After visiting Palestine in 2002 on behalf of the International Parliament of Writers and at the invitation of Palestinian poet Mahmoud Darwish, these writers released widely publicised witness accounts of the unspeakable horrors of American-funded Israeli state terrorism in the region. They were all roundly condemned and insulted by the Western media, the so-called bastions of free speech.[12]

The exclusions generated by the territorialisation of oppression can also provide useful analytical approaches to much of the ethnically driven socio-political problems that have become an almost permanent albatross of many postcolonial African societies, especially in terms of the constant tensions between specific ethno-cultural groups and the state in Africa. The example of the Igbo people of south-eastern Nigeria will suffice to buttress this assertion. Two major forms of postcolonial dysfunctionality characterise the nation-space that emerged as Nigeria after political independence was obtained from Britain in October 1960. On the one hand is the neocolonial peonage of the country to the forces of a globalised monopolist capitalism; on the other is the far more pernicious incidence of internal colonialism spelt out in the form of an ethno-religious will to dominance by the numerous ethnic nationalities violently welded together by the British without any consideration for specific historical trajectories.

The ethno-religious unit – ethnicity and religion can hardly be divorced in Nigeria and much of Africa – that controls the all-powerful federal government at the centre has almost always behaved as a domestic coloniser in the Nigerian context. The Hausa-Fulani in the Islamic north have been the dominant power holders since independence. It is against this backdrop of internal colonialism that Igbo questions can be properly analysed. The Igbo are the dominant ethnic group in eastern Nigeria, but within the country's broader geopolitical history they have been so thoroughly worsted as to constitute a conscience problem for the Nigerian polity. The Igbo have been victims of repeated genocides in northern Nigeria since the 1960s. And a major consequence of the secessionist attempt they made in 1967 has been an almost permanent exclusion of that ethnic group from the commanding heights of the Nigerian political process at the centre. This is the precise point at which problems of territorialisation and particularisation of oppression emerge in a patently Orwellian dimension.

Of all the elements – psychic, religious, cultural, political, linguistic – that can be identified as foundational to and constitutive of the postcolonial identity of the Igbo subject, the narrative of Igbo oppression and persecution by the Nigerian polity stands out. As a people, the Igbo do not have a singular history, religion, or culture, but Igbo leaders and intellectuals have been able to forge an overarching discourse of identity rooted in a collective sense of persecution and victimhood. The exceptionalist imaginary into which he or she is socialised makes it difficult for the contemporary Igbo subject to envisage an identity devoid of emotions of permanent victimhood within Project Nigeria. Here is a press report on a lecture delivered by Odumegwu Ojukwu, a respected Igbo politician and leader of the secessionist bid, in which he articulates an Igbo identity:

> Lamenting again the plight of the Igbo in the country's socio-economic and political setting, the Ikemba Nnewi, Chief Odumegwu Ojukwu yesterday said that thirty-two years after the Civil War, the Igbo still remain an endangered species. Ojukwu spoke in Owerri while delivering a lecture titled 'Nation Building in Nigeria: Lessons of Civil War' during a workshop organised by a German group, the Konrad Adenauer Foundation. He stated that the Igbo have always been victims of any sectarian/ethnic clash in Nigeria, decrying that till now, no Igbo man has been able to take the burden of leading the course of emancipation of his people ... Ojukwu added: *'When a Yorubaman quarrels with an Igbo, the Igboman gets killed, when the Hausa quarrels with the Yoruba, Igboman is killed, when Igboman quarrels with Hausa, Igboman is killed. It has even reached the stage*

*that the Palestinians will fight with Jews, the Igboman is
killed. What are we doing?'* he queried. Ojukwu added that
Ndigbo were facing a major national threat, stressing that
the time has come for an Igbo Presidency. 'The question of
Nigeria is nationhood. There is no balance in Nigeria if an
Igboman does not become president of Nigeria in 2003.'[13]

Ojukwu's discourse, and indeed much of Igbo discourse in
the Nigerian context, is energised by the same logic behind
Jewish and African American narratives of oppression: the
territorialisation of oppression and the investment of that
space with a people's history, emotions, and sensitivity; an
almost programmatic hostility toward other narratives of
oppression within the same space; and, ultimately, an Orwellian
hierarchisation of competing narratives of oppression. In the
portion of his speech that I italicised, it is no accident that
Ojukwu carefully avoids stating what happens when an Igbo
man quarrels with an Ijaw person, an Isoko person, an Itsekiri
person, an Ibibio person, or an Ogoni person.

Such a perspective would translate to an engagement of the
no less significant narratives of the oppression of the several
minority ethnic groups who share the south-eastern Nigerian
region with the dominant Igbo ethnic group. That would have
done serious damage to the exceptionalism of the Igbo narrative
of suffering and persecution, as it would mean admitting that
all the other minority ethnicities in that region have tales of woe
within the Nigerian system. It would have undone the thesis of a
rigid, never-changing, ontological victimhood that is so crucial
to the Igbo narrative. It would have shown that, in certain other
contexts and historical junctures, the Igbo can become – and
have been – the dominant oppressor group.

Although they felt betrayed by the fact that Ken Saro-
Wiwa opted for the federal side during the Nigerian civil war,
Wiwa's famously frosty relationship with the Igbo can also be

viewed through the prism of the threat that his later minority rights crusade posed to the exceptionalist construction of Igbo persecution within the Nigerian polity. Subsumed within his greater crusade of challenging the might of an oppressor – the Nigerian federal government and Western oil conglomerates – was another task of drawing attention to the plight of the ethnic minorities of south-eastern Nigeria, a space in which the Igbo constitute the dominant group. Wiwa's crusade, which he successfully internationalised, drew powerful attention to the fact that there were other oppressed peoples besides the Igbo in Nigeria. It drew attention to the fact that Nigeria is made up of so many layers of oppression as to render any rigid, Orwellian exceptionalism thoroughly problematic. And, as I have argued, dominant narratives of oppression, in their most radical, intolerant strands, can hardly live with any perceived violation of the 'territorial integrity' of their oppression by other contending narratives.

A people's oppression always exists in its undeniable, concrete materiality. That much is true of all the scenarios of oppression all over Africa. But the discourses generated on account of that oppression behave, all too often, like the 'Africa' of Abioseh Nicol's famous poem 'The Meaning of Africa':

> We look across a vast continent
> And blindly call it ours.
> You are not a country, Africa,
> You are a concept,
> Fashioned in our minds, each to each,
> To hide our separate fears
> To dream our separate dreams.
> Only those within you who know
> Their circumscribed plot,
> And till it well with steady plough
> Can from that harvest then look up

To the vast blue inside
Of the enamelled bowl of sky
Which covers you and say
'This is my Africa' meaning
'I am content and happy.
I am fulfilled, within,
Without and roundabout ...'

When an African intellectual denies a Québecois the right to express a particular form of oppression integral to his own history, when radical Igbo intellectuals stage discourses of oppression marked by an exceptionalist ideology that turns oppression into a sacrosanct space whose territorial integrity must be protected at the expense of other equally valid narratives of oppression, what we are faced with, beyond the undeniable materiality of the oppressions in question, are discursive behaviours in which oppression, like Nicol's Africa, becomes a 'concept, fashioned in our minds, each to each, to hide our separate fears'. This process, as I have shown, usually eventuates in those tragedies that have become so banal in Africa largely because of their continental ubiquity.

6

MAKWEREKWERE

The letters came within two days of each other. The first was an invitation from Professor Georges Hérault, director of the research wing of the French Institute of South Africa (IFAS). Three years after my first visit to South Africa in 1997 to assess the perception of francophone African literatures in that country's universities, IFAS was again inviting me as a visiting scholar. The second letter was from Chris Dunton, the well-known British professor of African literatures who is now chair of the English department of the National University of Lesotho at Roma. Dunton was inviting me to Lesotho as a visiting scholar to present a faculty of arts guest lecture. I arranged a few other engagements and braced myself for a very engaging psychic reconnection with the African continent.

I needed the return to Africa badly. I had been away from that continent for an uncomfortable stretch, carrying out my scholarly labour in the minefield of North American academia, writing Africa 'from a rift', as the Cameroonian Achille Mbembe would put it. I also needed the trip for other reasons.

I needed a break from the oppression of the image: the North American media image of Africa. The African living in North America is in constant danger of accepting whatever image of Africa s/he is presented with by the media as gospel truth. In North America, I have been consistently assailed, assaulted, and oppressed with images of Africa traceable to the colonial library: Africa-as-AIDS, Africa-as-hunger, Africa-as-civil-war, Africa-as-corruption, Africa-as-the-antithesis-of-democracy, Africa-as-everything-we-are-glad-not-to-be. You get tired of the ritual of explaining to charmingly ignorant interlocutors that there is a fundamental distinction between the Africa they see on CNN and the real Africa.

I also wanted a break from occidentalism. Fernando Coronil, the thinker who coined this term, takes great pains to explain that it is not the reverse of Edward Said's orientalism. Coronil uses the newer concept to account for those usually innocuous processes through which Westerners turn your racial and cultural difference into hierarchy and reproduce existing stereotypes about you in the process. Occidentalism covers all the mundane daily scenarios during which the Western world constantly reminds the immigrant of his or her otherness, strangeness, and difference:

'Oh, I love your accent. It's awesome. Where is that from?'
'Nigeria.'
'Nigeria? You mean Nicaragua?'

This often-repeated, seemingly innocent 'compliment' is usually the beginning of encounters that inevitably remind the immigrant that he or she does not belong.

Departure date finally came around. 'Be careful. Urban violence is rife in South Africa,' the Nigerian friends who drove me to the Vancouver airport warned. I shrugged and dismissed their anxiety. There may be violence in South Africa, but I certainly was not going to be scared of returning to Africa. I wasn't going to be afraid of black people in Africa!

I arrived in Johannesburg on a cold July morning. A delighted Georges Hérault was at the airport to welcome me. We drove straight to the IFAS offices in the downtown area of Johannesburg. After signing my research contract papers and meeting some of the new members of the research team, I announced to Hérault that I was going to take a stroll in the streets around IFAS. I was eager to get a feel of the same streets I had seen three years earlier. Hérault's countenance changed. 'Be careful,' he said. 'Don't go out there with your wallet. You could get mugged.' I assured Hérault I would be all right but took the precaution of leaving my valuables in his office.

I started my walk, my reconnection with African soil, on the busy Bree Street. As someone who had walked the same street three years earlier, I could not help but observe the heavy black presence. As is true of the Hillbrow area, blacks have taken over downtown Johannesburg. The official principle of separate development through which racial segregation was enforced under apartheid seems to have been replaced by what one may call an unofficial principle of voluntary separation. While separate development instituted an order in which blacks had to move out whenever whites moved in, as was the case in Sophiatown, voluntary separation now induces whites to move out quietly whenever and wherever blacks move in. Downtown Johannesburg is a vivid example of a space in which this new South African drama is being played out. This space, which was still predominantly white during my first visit, has now been taken over by blacks. In large office complexes and shopping malls, one does not fail to notice the ubiquitous 'To Let' signs, evidence of white retreat to other 'safe' areas of the city such as Rosebank or back 'home' to Britain, Holland, Canada, New Zealand, or Australia.

I stopped for a light lunch at a KFC outlet, my mind actively taking in the new realities. I finished my lunch and went back to walking the streets. I was about to cross a busy intersection when a street sign told me that I was on Fox Street. Fox Street! I had heard a lot of terrifying things about that street since my last trip to South Africa. It is said to be one of the most violent streets in Johannesburg. One could get mugged or killed for as little as a hundred South African rands. I looked around me anxiously. I was surrounded by a sea of inscrutable black faces. I touched my forehead and found out, much to my irritation, that I was perspiring profusely. It was winter in South Africa! And to my utter embarrassment, I discovered that I relaxed and felt safer each time white faces appeared in the crowd.

Here was I, a black man, looking anxiously for white faces to feel safe from black violence in an African city! And to think that back in Canada, I had dismissed insinuations that I could be scared of 'black violence' in South Africa! I reluctantly came to the realisation that I was far more affected by the oppression of the image than I had been willing to admit. The image of the post-apartheid black condition in South Africa is constantly constructed in the Western media around the problem of violence. Such stereotypical and prejudicial representations of black South Africa always employ two constantly repeated, over-sensationalised buzzwords: *mugging* and *robbery*. That image had quietly slipped into my subconscious and was responsible for my feeling so uneasy amidst my own racial kind on a busy street in Johannesburg. I hurried back to IFAS.

On hearing that I had arrived in Johannesburg, Professor Harry Garuba came from his base at the University of Cape Town to spend a weekend with me. As Harry and I hadn't seen each other since 1996, we had a riotously joyful reunion. The following day, we hit town. Harry wanted to see downtown Johannesburg. He also needed to go to the Consulate-General of Nigeria in Rosebank. As we meandered our way through the ever-busy Bree Street, Harry could not help observing how filthy downtown Johannesburg had become. I had made the same disturbing observation myself the day I arrived but had been reluctant to accept the disturbing fact that decay of public infrastructure seems to be the story in areas of the city inhabited by blacks. Predominantly black areas have become an eyesore. The beautiful lawns and flowerbeds I noticed in some areas three years earlier now tell sad stories of degradation. Some of them have become open-air urinals. Harry and I were worried. We tried to place ourselves in the shoes of white South Africans discussing the now filthy streets of Hillbrow and downtown Johannesburg: 'Ah, the good old days of apartheid!'

When Harry concluded his business at the Nigerian consulate, we took a bus and headed back to Georges Hérault's residence. I still don't know what it was about us that gave us away as foreigners, but the other passengers, all blacks, lapsed into an uneasy silence as soon as we boarded. I looked at the faces around us and thought I saw hostility. The tension in the air was so thick you could cut it with a knife. Harry confirmed my worst fears when we left the bus. I had just experienced, first-hand, South African xenophobia and I was to experience it again and again throughout my three-month sojourn in that country. Harry explained to me – with the coolness of someone used to it – that the black South African passengers on the bus had identified us as *makwerekwere*, hence the naked hostility. *Makwerekwere* is the derogatory term used by black South Africans to describe non-South African blacks. It reminds one of how the ancient Greeks referred to foreigners whose language they did not understand as the *barbaroi*. To the black South African, *makwerekwere* refers to black immigrants from the rest of Africa, especially Nigerians. I was confounded by the fact that black South Africa had begun to manufacture its own kaffirs so soon after the end of apartheid.

As I later discovered after a series of encounters, black South Africans have found an easy explanation for the myriad problems of poverty, housing, transportation, unemployment, crime, violence, and decay of public and social infrastructure.

'Ah, the *makwerekwere*! These Nigerians are all criminals! When they are not busy trafficking drugs, they are taking over our jobs, our houses, and, worse, our women. All foreigners must leave this country!' What Salman Rushdie refers to as a 'demonising process' of the Other is at work in South Africa and the consequences are predictably disastrous. There is so much anger and frustration among the Nigerians I met in South Africa. Most of them have become paranoid, living permanently in fear. In a discussion with some Nigerian medical doctors in Pretoria, I observed that their anger is directed mostly at black South African leaders. 'Imagine these South Africans treating us like this. They think apartheid came to an end because they fought in Sharpeville and Soweto. It means Mandela never told them the truth. Mbeki never told them the truth.'

The doctors were referring to Nigeria's heavy moral, political, and financial investment in the anti-apartheid struggle. Nigeria's financial and political commitment to that cause was total and unflinching. In the 1970s and 1980s, the South African freedom struggle was completely woven into Nigeria's national imaginary, so much so that a Nigerian leader, Olusegun Obasanjo, suggested we mobilised 'African juju' and other maraboutic forces of African sorcery to attack Pieter Botha and free our black brothers in South Africa. And he wasn't joking. Every Nigerian musician, from reggae singers to fuji musicians in the Yoruba tradition, waxed radical anti-apartheid lyrics to energise the 1970s and 1980s. 'Who owns the land, who owns the land? We want to know who owns Papa's land,' crooned Sonny Okosuns. Majek Fashek, the reggae man replied: 'Now, now, now, Margaret Thatcher, free Mandela.' Victor Essiet of The Mandators screamed: 'Truth is our right, Jah is our might, we must free South Africa!'

Everywhere you turned in the Nigeria of those heady decades, freedom for black South Africans was the dominant national agenda. Black South Africans, including President Thabo

Mbeki and Ezekiel Mphahlele, found warmth, hospitality, and friendship during their years of exile in Nigeria. Many black South Africans attended Nigerian universities on Nigerian scholarships. When it became clear that South African whites, like their European and American kinsmen, were determined to make peaceful change impossible and violent change inevitable, Nigerians donated financially to the armed struggle. I personally recall giving money during special anti-apartheid fund-raisers as a high school student in Nigeria. In view of this, the Nigerians I met in South Africa had only two words to describe the attitude of black South Africans to them: collective amnesia.

Prejudice has been the force majeure of so much of human history. Our pantheon of small-minded hate is formidable: Christian prejudice manufactured the unbeliever; Islamic prejudice manufactured the infidel; heterosexual prejudice manufactured the faggot; patriarchal prejudice manufactured the hysteric; European prejudice manufactured the native; American prejudice manufactured the nigger; German prejudice manufactured the Jew; Israeli prejudice manufactured the Araboushim; Afrikaner prejudice manufactured the kaffir. Not to be outdone, black South Africa has manufactured the *makwerekwere* as its unique post-apartheid contribution to this gory pantheon of hate. The joy of your instant-mix Nescafé or your instant-mix powdered milk is the considerable labour and hassle it saves you. Just pour water, add sugar to taste, and your drink is ready. The *makwerekwere* is black South Africa's instant-mix kaffir, very easily produced with minimum labour.

7

GOING TO MEET BLACK AMERICA

I met black America for the first time in 2005, after three years of living and teaching in the United States, and one year before I returned to Canada. The long journey to this eventful meeting began in my father's library in Isanlu. I came of age in Nigeria as the locust decades of military despotism and civilian kleptocracy set in, destroying everything – including what used to be known as the middle class. This class comprised a proud and hopeful generation that returned home from Cambridge, Oxford, Canterbury, Yale, Princeton, and Harvard in the euphoric 1960s–1970s. After years of colonial humiliation in the hands of the British, a newly independent and proud Nigeria beckoned and members of this new generation answered enthusiastically. 'Unity and Progress', 'One Nigeria', and other such soporific mantras were on their lips as they fanned across the land, taking up jobs in every sector of national life. Those who joined the education sector took up positions in the universities; some joined high schools founded and run by Western Christian missions; some others joined public elementary schools all over the country.

Those who accepted teaching positions in rural missionary schools brought the once vibrant national culture of the family library with them to our villages. My father belonged in this category. Being more Catholic than the Pope, he had hurried home from Dundee University in Scotland to be principal of a Catholic high school in Isanlu. Over the years, as our leadership transformed the Nigerian state into carrion and turned one of the world's richest geographies into Africa's most embarrassing atrophy, my siblings and I would harass him no end for that 'ill-considered' decision: 'Dad, why couldn't you just wait for the three of us to be born in the UK before rushing home?' We were in secondary school and could not understand why he denied us British citizenship. For most Nigerians of my generation, holding the passport of one Western country in addition to a Nigerian passport, evidence of dual citizenship, is a vital form of insurance. Whenever the Nigerian state defaults on its responsibilities to you as a citizen, your second citizenship kicks in to save the day. But Dad didn't wait for us to be born in the UK. He returned to Nigeria with his books and a wife pregnant with his first child.

That family library became his most important asset. He continued to expand it until he died in February 2007 and it became my most significant inheritance. I was practically raised in that library. There was nothing my father enjoyed more than having me, his last-born child and only son, spend hours with him there during my formative years. When we weren't reading, he was giving me long lectures on the value of knowledge, fulminating against the one thing he couldn't tolerate: 'a mind that has not read books', to put it in his words. And by books he meant 'serious books'.

Thus, while my secondary school mates enjoyed the delights of 'soft' literature – James Hadley Chase, Nick Carter, Frederick

Forsyth, and the Macmillan Pacesetters series – I was stuck in my father's library in the company of 'serious writers'. His vigilance, however, could not stop my underground addiction to Hadley Chase! Years later, I discovered the thematic thoroughness of my father's acquisitions: shelves of West African literature and history led to shelves of South African literature and history, which in turn yielded to shelves of African American literature and history. Colonialism. Apartheid. Slavery. These were the three great themes that informed his systematic acquisitions in black textual cultures as his library grew to take up two large rooms in the family house.

This was the beginning of my ensorcellment by the great texts of the black world. It was in this library that I encountered the names that would plunge me into an intricate web of trajectories and experiences that, years later, Paul Gilroy would famously call the Black Atlantic. From my senior years in secondary school and onward, my father's library ensured that names like Frederick Douglass, Ralph Ellison, W.E.B. Du Bois, Countee Cullen, Alain Locke, Langston Hughes, Claude McKay, Richard Wright, James Baldwin, Chester Himes, Stokely Carmichael, Booker T. Washington, Martin Luther King Jr., and Malcolm X entered my world in that small village in the middle of Nigeria. Whenever Mom complained that some of the stuff was just too high for my level, Dad would quip dismissively that at my age Catholic missionaries had already introduced him to Latin texts!

What university training added to this foundation was a transcendental, borderless black world that privileged colour, history, and memory above geography and nation. Thus, apartheid and slavery were also very much 'our experience', 'our property' in those undergraduate lecture rooms in Nigeria. The curriculum socialised us into treating histories and narratives specific to black South Africans and African Americans as phatic links to our own major narrative: colonialism. Our professors created a world of ideological intermeshing in which W.E.B Du Bois, Malcolm X, Richard Wright, James Baldwin, and Toni Morrison were as much 'our writers' as were Frantz Fanon, Walter Rodney, Wole Soyinka, Chinua Achebe, and Ben Okri. Years later, the strictures of disciplinary boundary-cutting in North American academe, the exigencies of national identities, and the fractious politics and tensions of intra-black relations would unsettle this seamless but soporific black world that I brought to the New World from Africa.

After completing a doctorate in Canada in 2002, I was hired by Penn State University. That was the beginning of my American odyssey. State College, Pennsylvania, is one of those typical American college towns where everything revolves around an octopus university. Rich, serene, beautiful, and almost always completely white, many American college towns have an invisible sieve that lets in just the right quota of *a certain kind* of yellow, brown, and black skin. Just enough dosage of coloured skin to enable the authorities to make politically correct noises about diversity and multiculturalism. Strategic tokenism. That certain kind of coloured skin is almost always a student or faculty member already mainstreamed and stabilised as non-threatening to America's whiteness.

Thus, my 'black' world in Pennsylvania comprised African and African American faculty and students, some of whom became family. Outside of that immediate circle was the broader circle of Nigerian writers and artists of my generation – we all moved to North America in the great haemorrhage of the 1990s. I spent alternate weekends with the writers Ogaga Ifowodo and Akin Adesokan in Ithaca, the painters Victor Ehikhamenor and Victor Ekpuk in Maryland, or the novelists Maik Nwosu and E.C. Osondu in Syracuse. The poet Obi Nwakanma made infrequent visits to our axis from his base in Missouri.

In the spring of 2005, I co-taught a funded graduate seminar in African and African American drama with Professor

Charles Dumas, an African American actor-professor who has featured in a good number of Hollywood films and also makes appearances in the television drama *Law and Order*. We had enough grant money to take the entire class to stage productions of black plays in Washington, D.C., Philadelphia, and New York. Towards the end of the semester, we got word that an August Wilson play was on at the Yale Repertory Theatre. Charles could not come along, so I had to drive the entire class of about ten white students to New Haven, Connecticut. It wasn't long into the play before I realised to my horror that I didn't understand anything the African American actors were saying. Not a word! I strained and stretched my ears to no avail. This was pure Ebonics. The sort of fast-paced American black English that always stands between me and one of my favourite comedians, D.L. Hughley. This, however, was my first blood-and-flesh contact with Ebonics. None of my African American brothers and sisters used it to interact with me in our cocooned sphere in academia.

As my frustration mounted, I had to rely on my students to whisper things to me. What's he saying? What's she saying? I kept asking. Then another shocking realisation: here was a black professor asking his white students to interpret and make sense of black actors for him! Suddenly, the Atlantic Ocean and the four centuries that stood between the African American and me were no longer the stuff of literature and history books or scholarly discourse. There it was inside that theatre, the tragic separation, requiring the separator to serve as bridge and reconnect what s/he separated! In Yale of all places!

This jolting contact with non-academic, non-mainstreamed African American idiom was only the first of a series of events that would take me to black America, away from the ostracism of academia. Shortly after the incident at Yale, I received an invitation from an old Nigerian friend who had made it to America on a diversity visa lottery and was living in Staten Island,

New York. As we hadn't seen each other in years, I wrote down his address and promised to spend an entire weekend with him. The trouble with MapQuest is that it takes you to a specific doorstep without telling you anything about the sociology of the neighbourhood. As I approached my friend's address after a six-hour drive from Pennsylvania, I got an eerie sense of the familiar. Apart from the fact that I was familiar with the ghetto in West Africa and had visited South African townships, years of reading African American writing and watching media stereotypes of the 'hood', especially blaxploitation films, had given me a fairly good mental picture of America's black ghetto. Could my Nigerian friend possibly be living in the ghetto? Everything around me looked very much like the mental image I had of the 'hood'.

My suspicions were confirmed when I pulled up in front of my friend's huge apartment complex. He was waiting for me in front of the building and rushed to my car as soon as he saw me. We barely exchanged pleasantries before he exclaimed, 'You can't park here. I'll take you to a friend's place. You'll leave your car there and we'll come back here by bus.' I let him in beside me in front. 'What's the problem?' I asked. 'You didn't tell me you drive a brand-new Toyota Camry!' he said. He explained that my car could attract hostility from folks in the neighbourhood. I was bewildered and it showed on my face. He explained that the idea of successful continental Africans coming to flaunt their success didn't always go down well. I got it. I'd read the literature about such areas of tension between continental Africans and the black community in America.

On the bus back to his place, I finally got to ask him why he was living there if things were that bad. His was a classic case of the ill-informed African giving up far better conditions back home for the American eldorado. On winning the diversity lottery visa, he gave up a good job in Lagos, sold his belongings, and headed to America only to discover that his Nigerian college of education diploma was meaningless. He moved from one odd job to another until he ended up as a security guard on Staten Island. He became friends with an African American co-worker who soon needed a room-mate to help with the rent, so he moved in. Since he did not join the American system at a level superior to the social and economic status of his room-mate and of most of the black folk in the neighbourhood, he reasoned that he was not a candidate for resentment and intra-racial backlash. 'But you,' he said, 'you are a professor and all that.'

I nodded and remarked that he had acquired some of the inflections and tonalities of Ebonics. I told him about my Yale experience. He laughed and confirmed that language had also been the most serious obstacle to his integration when he moved to that neighbourhood. His African American friends had trouble with his heavily accented Nigerian English but resented it when he confessed to having trouble with Ebonics. How could the brotha from Africa take on airs and pretend not to understand them? Things gradually smoothed out and he eventually blended and made very good friends. We arrived at his building and he led the way into the lobby. One look at my surroundings and my heart sank. The squalor! The squalor!

I have travelled extensively in Africa. I am familiar with all those spectacles of poverty and disease that Western voyeurs – journalists, missionaries, NGO experts, World Bank/IMF eggheads, etc. – love to present as 'Africa' to a Western audience high on its messianic self-image as the Great White Hope chosen by God to save the rest of us from ourselves. But nothing of what I'd seen anywhere in Africa prepared me for that jolting contact with American poverty and squalor. More scatological evidence of the black condition confronted me as we negotiated the long, dark, crowded, and grimy corridor leading to the two-bedroom apartment my host shared with his African American friend and co-worker. It turned out he had left out one significant detail: Rashonda, his room-mate's younger sister, was also crashing with them. Rashonda was a single mother with two young kids from two different men: a baby mama.

This was getting uncanny. Really. I had walked into a situation that assembled every imaginable American stereotype of the black community. Unfortunately, the mainstream America of gloss and chrome at the source of these stereotypes has never tried to project mentally into the black condition, let alone undertake a physical pilgrimage to the territory of this hidden and oppressed humanity. I was introduced to our African American hosts as a cousin visiting from Pennsylvania. By now, I'd learnt that my being a university professor was an inconvenient detail my Nigerian friend was reluctant to let out in these circumstances.

The sociology of interactions in that building and neighbourhood was Africa on display. People moved in and out of one another's spaces and apartments without the cold formalities that have emptied social interaction of all humanising value in the West. Shouts of 'Yo!' and 'Whaz up, ma nigga?' were ubiquitous. Four hundred years of violent separation from the source in Africa and they still *remembered* those modes of warmth. I became part of the toing and froing between apartments and spaces. My hosts took me to fraternise with 'otha brothas and sistas'. All the places I saw told the same story of roaches, rats, grime, overcrowding, drugs, despondency, and hopelessness. Anger. The black anger that surprised white America when the Reverend Jeremiah Wright treated them to an infinitesimal snippet of the smouldering crucible they have sat on and repressed for four hundred years. The black folk who received me so warmly were still saddled with the dud American cheque that Martin Luther King had complained about so many years ago. Some forty years after his death, they still cannot cash in on America's promise: insufficient funds.

No matter how hard I tried, I couldn't blend. They caught a whiff of the African continent the moment they saw me, even before my accent gave things away. Everywhere we went I was moved by the brotherhood and fellowship that was extended to me in the middle of so much poverty. We would gather in someone's apartment to drink and talk late into the night. I gave them Africa; they gave me a black America that until that moment had been for me the stuff of scholarly discourse and texts. A black America that has never gained access into the eyes, ears, and consciousness of white America.

I tried to teach them Nigerian pidgin English and they gave me lessons in Ebonics and black slang. Ultimately, the interactions revealed the damage wrought by the great historical chasm. The questions some of them asked me about Africa were simply unbelievable, as unbelievable as some of my own long-held facile assumptions about them. The divide-and-rule brainwash of America had inscribed Africa in their imagination as a better-forgotten oasis of original savagery. To them, Africa was a horrifying marriage of Hobbes (the state of nature) and Conrad (*Heart of Darkness*): 'Yo, dem folks have cars in Africa? Like here?' And they appeared so incredulous when my friend and I replied in the affirmative. My friend was elated. 'I told you so,' he gloated.

I tried as hard as I could to disentangle Africa: to present it to them as a diverse geography of some fifty-four countries as opposed to the homogenous, singular basket of savagery that America had woven into their imagination. As they told me about their own gory experiences in the America of the year 2005, I had to quickly unlearn my privileges and reduce my ignorance of the black experience in America. Unless you're a black person from white settlerist South Africa, Namibia, Zimbabwe, or Kenya, the mountain of daily racial oppressions and institutionalised discrimination that African Americans load into the expression 'white folk' may not resonate for you as fiercely and as urgently as it does for them. You may not start and end every sentence with 'white folk' and your interlocutors could get impatient with you. What, for you, has become colonial history is still, for them, painful daily reality.

As I drove back to Pennsylvania at the end of what had been a road-to-Damascus experience, my emotions oscillated between joy and sadness. I was glad that I had had the opportunity to meet black America outside the gloss of seminar rooms, conference venues, and the text. I was saddened by the realisation that I was not unlike so many other continental African intellectuals who spend decade after decade in America without ever going beyond the black America of the text, seminar rooms, and conference venues, and who often indulge in authoritative pronouncements on the African American condition. We make friends with African American colleagues. Sometimes the friendship gets so strong we become family. Yet we hardly ever ask to be taken to the roots and routes they navigated to academe – and the mountains they overcame along the way. I realised I'd never been 'home' with any of my African American family. I was saddened by the observation of this grim disconnect.

Back in Pennsylvania, I phoned a cousin who was a student in Alabama. I told him that I needed a road trip in rural Alabama and Mississippi in the summer of 2005 to continue my education. He laughed and told me that what I mistook for black poverty in the state of New York was in fact black luxury! 'I will show you black poverty when you come to the South,' he said. He was right. We spent a whole month travelling in America's black poverty belt in the South. In certain places, it felt like the plantation was still alive and healthy. Only Massa was gone. Here were Americans poorer than anyone I have ever met in Africa. American towns and neighbourhoods more indigent than any place I'd seen in Africa. I travelled in those spaces where the anger that white America doesn't understand smoulders.

Today, as I listen to Barack Obama and John Edwards talk about the two Americas that need to be brought together, I marvel at the distance between their politician-speak and reality. Contrary to Obama and Edwards's theory, there are not two Americas. America is a minimum of four planets separated by a gulf of violence and unending injustice: a Hispanic planet, a Native American planet, a black American planet, and planet white America. The first three planets orbit around the blazing fourth which has narrativised itself as the sun. Although planet white America has been to the moon and is assiduously studying Mars preparatory to a visit within the next twenty years, it has never visited any of the three coloured planets right there under its nose. It doesn't even feel the need to project mentally onto those three planets – hence the shock with which it received the so-called anger of Jeremiah Wright.

The road to any meaningful contact between planet white America and the other American planets it has never met lies first and foremost in the desensitisation of the most sensitive body part in planet white America: the ears. The ears of planet white America are so sensitive that there are way too many truths it does not want to hear about the reality of America as lived and experienced daily by those on the coloured planets it has never visited. America's many inconvenient truths tend to hurt those ears, so it is better to repress them. Sensitive ears and repression of the inconvenient cost America lessons it could have learnt from Katrina and Jena. Jeremiah Wright's voice, screaming from the black planet, grated on those sensitive ears. What I learnt from my conversations with the black America that I met in the course of my education is the feeling that after recording successes in the civil rights struggle to be seen in America, black Americans are now simply never heard.

When those ears have been desensitised, America will also have to resolve the clash between memory and non-memory.

The history of America has evolved in such a way that planet white America either cannot afford the luxury of memory or can only tolerate the most doctored, sanitised memory that eventuates robotically in exceptional narratives of the world's only good country. Any contrarian memory, such as defines the trajectory and humanity of Jeremiah Wright and black America, is a dangerous threat to the orthodoxy of a neatly packaged national self-image. Until America resolves the clash between memory and its negation, the words of Ralph Ellison which I encountered years ago in the essay 'If the Twain Shall Meet' will always be waiting for her around the corner, just when she thinks she has turned that corner: 'It would seem that the basic themes of our history may be repressed in the public mind, but like corpses in mystery dramas, they always turn up again – and are frequently more troublesome.'

8

OF CATS AND CATRITUDE

Criss-crossing the circuits of knowledge and culture as an African in Euro-America entails the ability to manage confusion. Every African in the West is a CEO of a vast enterprise of cultural confusion. The confusion often stems from those slippery identity situations when you are called to manage multiple definitions of the self as an African. The catch, of course, is that you are never the author of any of those identities. They are authored for you almost as preconditions for your residency in the West. Hence, in my more than a decade of circulation in Euro-America, I've had to learn to listen to the West and know when it summons me to perform any of my identities: African, Nigerian, Yoruba, Catholic-Christian male. Sometimes, the occasion requires you to be all of these identities at once. Other occasions require a combination of some of them.

Sometimes, some of these identities face the threat of outright erasure, especially in academic contexts of cultural canonisation, whenever the West determines that they have outlived their usefulness. Examples of identity that were exposed to clear and present danger as soon as I began to move in the circuits of North American cultural discourse – they call it postmodernism when it pertains to the Western/white world and postcolonialism when it pertains to the non-Western/coloured world – were the noun *Africa* and the adjective *African*. Despite all the crises that still pit people against people, communities against communities, and villages against villages in Africa; despite wars; despite divisions; despite poverty, hunger, and disease, Africans still tend to instinctively believe in transcendental cultural commonalities, ways of seeing and being that we believe establish our common Africanness and distinguish us from the rest of humanity. We love to think of hospitality and warmth as distinctive markers of our African identity. We speak of African communalistic ethos as opposed to the individualistic ethos encountered in other cultures and civilisations.

Not so fast, says the North American cultural discourse industry. When you say you are African, it's too vague, too transcendental, too essentialist. You have to qualify and contextualise it. And what is this general Africa you keep referring to anyway? That too is essentialist. It dawns on you that this has become a problem when your manuscripts and articles are returned to you with comments and 'suggestions for improvement and revision' that ask you to qualify your use(s) of Africa by making it (them) more specific. Suddenly, because of the suffocating influence of North American high theory over the global production of meaning and identity, you get to call yourself African and talk about Africa in broad, generic terms only after entering countless caveats and precautionary notes.

Why was it possible to talk broadly of Africa and Africans until North American postmodernity and postcoloniality decided that the game was up? The imperative of a coordinated response to the violence of Euro-modernity provided the justification for the production of the transcendental and overarching Africa we encountered in all major twentieth-century identity projects and narratives such as pan-Africanism, nationalism, Negritude, and decolonisation. This transcendental Africa, which early Negritude discourse romanticised as 'Mother Africa', found its most engaging presentation in the pages of the journal *Présence Africaine*.

The politics and imperatives of the time led to the immediate emergence of a transnational, engagé crop of nationalists, statesmen, public intellectuals, literati, and culturati in the first half of the twentieth century who could criss-cross continental and international boundaries of discourse and politics, wearing the toga of a transcendental identity as the African intelligentsia. Although subsequent developments such as the dynamics of decolonisation, Cold War neocolonialist intricacies, and the emergence of the nation-state would subsequently subsume their identities within the national, there remains a sense in which the likes of Alioune Diop, Kwame Nkrumah, Jomo Kenyatta, Nnamdi Azikiwe, Sékou Touré, and Julius Nyerere continue to occupy a certain discursive space in which their transcendental identity as African statesmen and intelligentsia remains unimpeachable.

That this notion of a free-floating, transcendental Africa crossed the Atlantic and animated discursive energies in early disciplinary Africanist work in North America is not in doubt. It also true that this model has now become so discredited that any recourse to a transcendental Africa – or African identity – now automatically faces serious problems of institutional and disciplinary legitimacy. Indeed, African scholars and writers located in North America are sometimes the first to rush to town, discrediting such usages of a transcendental African identity as insensitive to the local, the particular, and the specific. The South African does not want to be thrown into the same basket of Africanness with 'those criminal Nigerians'. The Eritrean believes that Ethiopia will always come first in any general categorisation that does not specifically mention and valorise Eritrea.

While we now generally write about multiple little, local, and regional Africas in response to North American institutional and disciplinary pressures on engagements of the continent, I have lately become troubled by the fact that we have accepted the situation as a fait accompli, a precondition for the institutional validation of our work. We hardly bother to examine how we got here – where the rain began to beat us, as Chinua Achebe would put it. I want to propose a few explanations, albeit from the perspective of an academic who has been writing Africa from a North American location for a little over a decade.

The road to the breakdown of Africa into little consumable and digestible units in North American academia started, in a sense, with the scramble for and the appropriation of French theory. The scenario is sufficiently familiar: the North American institutional establishment found itself reduced to a megaphone in a curious division of labour that consecrated France as the producer of original thought. Claude Lévi-Strauss, Michel Foucault, Jacques Lacan, Gilles Deleuze, Jacques Derrida, Jean Baudrillard, Luce Irigaray, Hélène Cixous, Julia Kristeva, and Pierre Bourdieu became subjects of the great North American scramble for French theory from the 1960s onwards. Enter Jean-François Lyotard with his postmodernist credo of incredulity towards totalisations and grand narratives! After two disastrous wars, the Western world had grown tired of the Frankenstein it created: the White Male and his five hundred years of delusional self-narration as Reason, Rationality, Civilisation, and Progress. This apathy is what Lyotard puts with so much brio into those memorable words 'incredulity towards metanarratives' in *La condition postmoderne*.

Lyotard's suggestion that we move away from totalities came at a time when polymaths like Edward Said, Gayatri Spivak, Homi Bhabha, and Africa's Anthony Appiah were already taking the West to task for the largely undifferentiated, monolithic Others it produced in the locations of historical conquest.

Postcolonial theory, postmodernism, and cultural theory were on the march, de-totalising and breaking down everything in sight – especially any sense of an overarching Africa or a transcendental African identity. These new discourses exercised such a nightmarish stranglehold on the North American knowledge industry that they were even allowed the luxury of their own law enforcement agency: the essentialism police! In the United States and Canada, the fear of essentialism became the beginning of institutional wisdom and the open sesame to disciplinary validation and relevance.

Suddenly I am no longer allowed to be African for more than five minutes in a single day just because I move in the discursive circuits of the postcolonial and the postmodern. With their excessive fear of any form of stability, these discourses traffic in such keywords as contingency, shifts, flux, and tentativeness. Culture and any kind of identity is provisional, contingent, constantly shifting, and must be continuously negotiated and renegotiated. In the nature of things, I am allowed to be Nigerian in the morning, African at noon, black diasporic subject in the afternoon, and African or black male in the evening. If I tarry too long in any of these identity locations, the essentialism police will be on hand to remind me of the dangers of totalisation and stabilised identities. And if I dare speak of transcendental African commonalities between Paul Tiyambe Zeleza and me, that would be sacrilege. I would have occluded our differences as nationals of different African countries.

The most problematic consequence of this new politics of knowledge production and new ways of writing Africa has been so surreptitious in its workings that very few African intellectuals are mindful of it. Part of the long-term project of postcolonial discourse has been to question narratives – Western and African – that are deemed to fix Africa as a permanent, unchanging victim of the West and its violent modernity. The category of the colonised has enjoyed particular attention from postcolonial thinkers. In thesis after thesis, we are told that one fundamental flaw in early anti-colonial writing, say, Fanon's *The Wretched of the Earth*, Chinweizu's *The West and the Rest of Us*, and Rodney's *How Europe Underdeveloped Africa*, is that the colonised is described as an unchanging victim of the West. We are told that fixing the colonised as victim ignores the rich histories of colonial ambivalence and initiatives of resistance on the part of the colonised all over Africa. We are told that power was variegated and multifaceted in the political topography of colonialism, and that the African in King Leopold's Congo was not merely a passive object, perpetually acted upon: s/he also acted, and our discursive work on Africa must unearth and record these little voices of history. So far so good.

The story gets a lot more interesting when we make a temporal shift into the so-called postcolonial present of multinational capitalism, transnationalism, and globalisation. We have been told by thinkers like Arjun Appadurai and Masao Miyoshi that the condition of this present age is characterised by global fluxes of unprecedented dimensions, the breakdown of national borders and the attendant undermining of the power of the nation-state, the rise of multinational corporations, the collapse of the traditional boundaries between metropole and periphery.

These factors, we are told, have led to the emergence of a 'new continent' of Third World immigrants in the West. To these we must add the gains of the information age and the global propinquities they occasion: YouTube can instantly bring a traditional Yoruba naming ceremony live into my North American cultural studies classroom. These fluxes and the constantly shifting positions that inhere in them, we are told, make it impossible to delineate a West that permanently oppresses and an Africa that is permanently oppressed. There are no permanent victim positions since everything is contingent, fluid, and constantly shifting. If there are no permanent victims, it follows, of course, that there is no permanent oppressor. It is therefore counterproductive to continue to think of the West as a permanent oppressor of Africa.

After all, contemporary Europe is different from the new global behemoth, the United States of America. What's more, 'Europe' has expanded significantly to include states that emerged after the collapse of the Soviet Union. Can Lithuania, Romania, and Latvia be conceptualised as part of a monolithic, unchanging West that is the permanent nemesis of Africa? The continuous recourse to the idea of a transcendental, oppressor-West in Africanist and other Third World discourses is, therefore, essentialist and wrong. The West needs to be unpacked and localised every time it is invoked.

Sound reasoning on the surface. However, dangers lurk when Africanist writing embraces this sort of postcolonialist and postmodernist rationalisation of our contemporary condition without seeking to understand who has a strategic interest in dissolving the difference between oppressor and oppressed, between victim and victimiser. Whose interest do these new ways of writing Africa serve ideologically and politically? When we are told that continuous recourse to colonialism as a causative explanation of some of Africa's present woes is tiring and counterproductive, when we are told to get over it and stop essentialising, who benefits from the erasure of our memory? In the North American context, why do postcolonial and postmodernist theorists become tongue-tied when they encounter the narratives of the Jewish community? Who is the postmodernist thinker that would assert, in the US, that Jewish recourse to and continuous instrumentalisation of the historical event of the Holocaust as an explanation of the Jewish present amounts to essentialism and entrapment in the past? Why is the case always different with Africa?

A trip to the Serengeti plain in East Africa will help me better illustrate the dynamics at work. For when we are told not to represent the West as a monolithic oppressor of Africa, when we are told not to essentialise Africa or what it means to be an African, there are dynamics at work depending on who is doing the talking! If you have access to a television, switch the channel to Animal Planet or the Discovery Channel. Jeff Corwin or the late Steve Irwin will be on hand to take you on a tour of the Serengeti with me. Perhaps you already know the story. Life in the Serengeti is not a tea party. It is an unending allegory of survival which, tragically, reflects the nature of human interactions in the last five-hundred-odd years. Access to and ownership of the means of survival is the name of the game in the Serengeti. Lions, cheetahs, leopards, and opportunistic hyenas are in constant competition for game and space. Sometimes game is plentiful and at other times there is famine. The natural pecking order is, of course, always respected. Antelopes, impalas, and zebras know their place in the food chain. They do their best to avoid the omnipresent predators.

Because of the nature of power, the story of the Serengeti always comes to us from the perspective of the big cats. They own the story and can shape it according to their will. Lately, the cats of the Serengeti have been unhappy. Led by the lions, they have been grumbling very loudly that the impalas have managed to come up with their own stories. What is more, these stories are patently unfair to the big cats. The impalas would have the whole world believe that they are permanent, never-changing victims in the order of things in the Serengeti!

Absent from the bizarre story of the impalas is the fact that the category of predator is not all-encompassing and transcendental. So essentialist is the story of the impalas that they are blind to the necessity of establishing ontological differences between lions, cheetahs, and leopards. Only bad faith and cynicism would make the impalas ignore the qualitative difference between being eaten by lions and being eaten by cheetahs. The two processes are different and cannot be levelled or essentialised into one master narrative of predation.

The lions are particularly angry. Apart from trying to accord a dubious transcendental fixity to their identity as predators in a questionable story that fixes the impalas as victims, the narrative of the impalas also glosses over the fact that the lions sometimes democratise oppression in the Serengeti by condescending to eat warthogs and even rabbits in lieu of impalas. The cheetahs of the Serengeti are even more furious. Absent from the story as narrated by the impalas – which seems to level all cats as predators – is the fact that some cats are more equal than others. After all, the cheetahs lose a high proportion of their kills to thieving lions and hyenas!

But the impalas are adamant. Their story is the only weapon they have. They find it terribly insulting to be told that there is a difference between being eaten by a lion and being eaten by a cheetah or a leopard. They find it exasperating to be told, it changes nothing about the transcendental, unchanging, and overarching catitude that is the source of their oppression in the Serengeti. And if impalas, antelopes, and zebras decide to valorise a collective, transcendental identity as victims of a transcendental, monolithic, and overarching catitude in the Serengeti, what makes such a narrative essentialist and unworkable? Who stands to gain if it is delegitimised?

Certainly, postcolonialist and postmodernist anti-essentialists in the North American academy, who would have us devote attention to the finer details of the differences between being colonised and oppressed by Europe and being neocolonised and oppressed by the United States in the context of the new world order, or who would have us hedge and endlessly qualify identities like 'Africa', 'African', and 'African woman', have a lot to learn from the impalas of the Serengeti. I should be able to claim a common Africanness with a Kenyan, a Cameroonian, and a South African without being accused of ignoring our differences.

9

ACCENT WARS

The internationally acclaimed African scholar and a long-time mentor of mine, Paul Tiyambe Zeleza, once came to Canada for a meeting in Montréal. Prior to his arrival from his US base, he had done things the African way by sending an email to notify me that he was coming to my neck of the woods in Canada. Could he tempt me to embark on the two-hour drive from Ottawa for a long-overdue reunion in Québec's leading city? He needn't have asked! Ever since we both left Penn State in 2005 – where the seeds of a mutually enriching brotherhood in Africanist intellection were sown – I have always looked forward to every opportunity of relinking with the mentor I fondly call *Mwalimu* (Teacher), the idea being to catch up on matters of mutual intellectual interest while getting our *beering* right!

Given the fact that our last meeting was in Ann Arbor at an African studies symposium back in April 2007, I wasn't going to miss the latest opportunity. I cleared my schedule and headed out to Montréal on a wet Saturday evening. The plan had been for me to arrive in time to also catch up with Professor Ato Quayson, another mentor who was attending the same event from Toronto. A combination of bad weather and horrible traffic ensured that I missed Ato. I arrived at the impressive Fairmont Le Reine Elizabeth – wondering what a monumental super-luxury hotel named after the head of a moribund, Anglo-colonialist monarchy was doing in that intensely Franco-nationalistic context of Québec, where everybody and everything that feels Anglo, looks Anglo, and sounds Anglo is a mortal enemy!

It was too late to have more than five minutes of riotous African reunion – complete with the joyful, expansive body gestures, raucous laughter, handshaking, and hugging, all vital elements in the atmospherics of 'African warmth' – with Paul. We agreed to meet the following morning for breakfast. Breakfast was everything one would expect in a well-appointed five-star hotel. Paul and I decided to celebrate our reunion with helpings from the sumptuous buffet breakfast in dignified quantities worthy of a trip to the bellies of two African men: sausages, omelettes, hash browns, buttered baguette, assorted fruits, plain yogurt, coffee and the like. Our overloaded plates looked attractive! The atmosphere was convivial, the sort that encouraged friendliness towards people seated at other tables.

He irrupted from nowhere, almost like an apparition. Tall. Heavily built. Ebullient. Scraggy beard on a scraggy sixtyish face. Brotherhood was in the air and it was obvious he wanted very much to be brotherly. 'Morning guys,' he wafted effusively, his huge frame casting an early morning aura on our table. Paul and I looked up, startled, and returned his greeting politely. 'So where are you guys from?' he asked. Paul and I tensed up a little bit. From experience. For the black person in Euro-American diaspora, that question is usually the beginning of a journey through an assembly line the final product of which could be unpleasant.

Often, too often, such questions come from folks, especially Western liberals, who mean well; who just want to be friendly and polite; who will tell you about their African American neighbour in the second sentence of the conversation; who will tell you about their African co-worker in the third sentence of the conversation; who will tell you about the safari they are planning to the Serengeti in the fourth sentence of the conversation – all in the bid to establish an 'I'm-with-you' résumé. In the ten seconds it took us to answer his question, I looked around furtively and discovered that Paul and I were the only black people eating in that restaurant. Until now it hadn't even occurred to us to notice that detail.

'From here,' Paul and I answered in perfect concert, as if planned. I took a quick mental note of our remarkable convergence of minds. If we were going to be othered, why make things easy for our newly minted brother? If the Westerner, pushed by a certain anthropological instinct to unearth the 'native' or 'tribal' roots of every black person s/he encounters in the Occident, has learnt to shoot without missing, we have equally learnt to fly without perching! We might as well indulge our new friend by taking him through the formula we were both so familiar with and were sure would guide the rest of the unfolding interaction. He half-smiled, half-frowned as expected and continued: 'I mean, where are you originally from?'

We would have been surprised if that formulaic question hadn't followed. 'Oh, I'm from Ontario,' replied Paul, who, after all, carries a Canadian passport. I opted to let Paul handle things here. Bringing my own Nigerian passport/origins into the picture would ruin the game. Our interlocutor appeared a tad uncomfortable, but his mask of generous smiles did a pretty good job of shielding the traces of redness that were beginning to appear on his face. He wasn't done yet. The liberal, well-meaning Occidental never gives up that easily. 'Really? You're from Ontario? Nice. I'm from Scotland. So what do you guys do here?'

'What do you do in Scotland?' I butted in at this point with my most expansive smile of the morning. 'I'm a farmer,' he offered. 'My daughter lives here in Canada and I try to visit once a year.' We didn't get to react to this family snippet before he took things to the next level. He looked at our plates and finally seemed to be aware for the first time that we were actually having breakfast. All it took was just a fraction of a second – he was a master of the quick comeback – for us to notice those ominous movements of facial muscles that are very often the loquacious abode of the unsaid and the unsayable in such circumstances: the imperceptible tweak around the corners of the mouth; the rapid flicker of the eyelids; the slight quiver of the eyebrows; then the smile and the statement that gives everything away: 'Hey, they serve a nice breakfast here, don't they? Are you guys enjoying this? Different from African food, eh?' As he spoke, he pointed obliviously in the direction of Paul's plate, the offending finger almost touching Paul's sausages and hash browns. He was that carried away.

We had not told him we were Africans!

Our friend's problem was finally outed. It was clear he had not set out for breakfast that morning expecting to find two folks like us making ourselves so comfortable in what, in his mind, was clearly not our 'natural environment'. Remember, it was the Fairmont Le Reine Elizabeth in Montréal, not the jungle! Worse, we were treating ourselves to a full complement of continental breakfast buffet that was apparently too civilised for our native palates!

Different from African food, eh?

And that rude finger in Paul's food! We both knew it was time to end the intrusion if we were not to lose our appetites. Allow a leper a handshake and he will take things to the next level by insisting on a bear hug. There was no way of telling if our ever-smiling friend would not politely ask if he could join our table and proceed to insist on a free anthropological lecture on African food. Words became unnecessary. The grave look on our faces told him to begin a dialogue with his legs. After all, the Yoruba have always claimed that the face is the abode of discourse. He mumbled something inaudible about the weather and left.

Paul and I joked about the situation. I remarked that the encounter with our friend was very good pedagogical material for some of those graduate seminars we teach in the production of otherness. Our mirth, however, did not in any way becloud the grave implications of what we had just experienced. I summed up the situation. Here was Paul Tiyambe Zeleza, one of the greatest and finest intellectual minds the African continent has to offer, having breakfast with a younger colleague. A half-illiterate farmer from remote Scotland casts one look at them and sees black, sees two signifyin' Bantus who had dared to venture out of the space he had assigned their ilk in his mind!

I drove back to Ottawa, my mind busy. The Scotsman had produced irresistible material for a new paper, possibly a lecture. I had to do something. Back in Ottawa, I drove straight to campus ... and to news of a tragedy. A rapist had struck on campus; a Caucasian student had been raped and brutalised. The whole campus was in crisis mode. Campus security and the Ottawa police had come up with a news alert that was posted everywhere on campus. Local radio and TV stations were also reading out the alert intermittently. I got to my nineteenth-floor office and went straight into my email.

The communications department of my university had sent out the police alert as a campus-wide email communiqué. The email contained the usual fare of information one is accustomed to on North American campuses in such circumstances. I read it, sympathised with the victim, and wondered how that could have happened in our otherwise serene and beautiful campus. My instinctive feeling of solidarity with the authors of the communiqué suffered an abrupt setback when I got to that part of the notice where they solicit my help – and the help of the entire university community – for information concerning the suspect. Hear them:

Description of Suspect:
White male
Height between 5'8" and 5'10" with broad shoulders and a chubby build in his mid-twenties
Bald head wearing a blue sweatshirt
Carrying a white Macy's bag
Spoke English with no accent

Spoke English with no accent? I suddenly began to miss our Scottish friend in Montréal. At least he had not taken occidental arrogance to the point of assuming, as do Canadians and their American brothers south of the border, that there are human beings on this wide planet of ours who speak English with no accent!

10

THE BOY FROM GHANA

The other day I was at a Ghanaian friend's place in Ottawa. He was a new acquaintance who had spent time in Nigeria in the 1970s and 1980s, before the incompetent civilian government of the day heaped the blame for all the country's woes on the Ghanaian diaspora in Nigeria and sent them packing. Ghana-must-go bags, widely used today by Nigerian politicians to steal and store raw cash, have become the most intriguing legacy of that collective demonisation of Ghanaians, as well as Nigeria's unique contribution to the global lexicon of corruption.

I had also spent time in Ghana – in Accra and Ho – in the early 1990s. Our experience of each other's countries provided fodder for cacophonous, brotherly African conversation, aided by Ghanaian delicacies and generous quantities of the abomination we call bottled palm wine here in North America. I recalled my time in Ghana: good roads, a stable electricity and water supply, efficient public service delivery at all levels, courtesy in government offices, security of life and property, extremely warm people, and, above all, ridiculous levels of corruption. I recalled the level of noise Ghanaians made if a politician was so much as suspected of having misappropriated, say, fifty thousand dollars. In Nigeria, a politician who steals as little as fifty thousand dollars could be found guilty not of stealing but of embarrassing the Nigerian state by the amount involved.

Politicians in the 'giant of Africa'[14] have evolved a culture of stealing 'giantly', in the hundreds of millions. And theft is denominated in US dollars. In Nigeria, it is not dignifying to steal in naira, the local currency. When Nuhu Ribadu, the anti-corruption czar, began to take his job too seriously, fighting corruption – even if selectively – rather than making the appropriate body language to convince the international community that Nigeria was indeed fighting corruption, he was promptly shoved aside. My Ghanaian friend made the familiar feel-good, consolation comments other concerned African brothers always make when Nigerians lament the fate of their country: These things happen everywhere, you know. Even in North America. It is not peculiar to Nigeria. Things were even worse in Ghana but we came out of the woods. Don't be fooled by the Ghana you experienced in the 1990s. We were in the doldrums before then. If Ghana can do it, Nigeria can do it …

Our discussion moved to football – the real football, not the hand-and-leg ball they call football in North America – and we almost brought down the roof as is customary when Africans discuss the continent's religion. That year's edition of the African Cup of Nations tournament was about to kick off in Ghana and I assured my friend that President Kufour[15] would be pleased to deliver the cup to the Nigerian captain, Nwankwo Kanu, at the end of the competition. Although they were lucky to beat us by only four goals in London the last time we had a friendly, Ghana, like Cameroon and Ivory Coast, are our junior brothers in football. My friend dismissed me as a typical Nigerian loudmouth.

We were about to place bets when his eight-year-old son stormed out of his bedroom screaming, 'Dad, turn on the Tee Vee!' My friend reached for the remote control and flicked on the television. The new commercial for Wendy's, the North American fast-food restaurant chain, was on. The lad asked: 'Dad, why do the tribesmen want to eat that innocent man?' A hush fell on us. The palm wine turned stale in my mouth. My friend looked at me in exasperation. I looked at him in exasperation. *Oro p'esi je*! All the answers one could have given the boy have been devoured by the question, as the Yoruba would exclaim in circumstances such as this. How do you explain the racial politics of Wendy's new commercial to an eight-year-old?

I had noticed that commercial when it first went on air and dismissed it as one of those irritating Western representations of the so-called natives. Little did I know that an eight-year-old Ghanaian boy would drive home its full tragic import. Desperate to become a household name like McDonalds and KFC, Wendy's had dug into the deepest recesses of the Western imagination to produce its latest TV advertisement. What's the gist of this offensive commercial? Roll tape: We are in the jungle. A bunch of cannibals appear with a prized prey, a Caucasian human being that they have ostensibly captured for dinner. He is attached to a pole slung over the shoulders of some of the cannibals. They are hurrying home to a good dinner.

The cannibals look fearful. They remind you of Chinua Achebe's description of masquerades in *Things Fall Apart*. They certainly remind me of Ojigindo, the fearful ancestral masquerade in my hometown, whose annual outing succumbed to the civilising mission of Roman Catholic priests when I was in elementary school. I now have only vague memories of Ojigindo, etched in my imagination as paganism until I encountered Negritude philosophy in my first year as an undergraduate in Nigeria. Wendy's cannibals are covered in chalk-white powder from head to toe. Their nakedness is covered only by skirts of reed. They carry spears and other primitive implements. The Caucasian pleads for his life in American English: 'Please don't eat me! I'm not delicious! I don't taste good.' He has a clear, definite identity as an American. The cannibals do not get any such treatment. They are not that lucky. They remain an open, vicious signified. They could be Africans, Native Americans, Maoris, or Aborigines. In short, anything but Western and modern.

They are not us but they want to eat us!

Eventually, one of the cannibals shows himself capable of reasoning and worthy of preliminary admission into Western modernity. Thankfully, the commercial endows him and his kinsmen the gift of native-speak, the sort of incomprehensible native babble you find in Conrad and Sir Rider Haggard. 'He is right, you know,' our cannibal pronounces in cannibal-speak, modernised and rendered in English as Wendy's subtitles flicker onto the screen. He then advises his fellow cannibals to dump the human prey and opt for any of the items on Wendy's delicious menu.

This was what caught the attention of my Ghanaian friend's eight-year-old son. The boy from Ghana naturally identified with the Caucasian victim and was horrified by the fact that the tribesmen almost ate an innocent man but for Wendy's felicitous and humanitarian intervention. I sympathised with my friend as he wrestled with what to tell an inquisitive boy. Do you tell an eight-year-old African boy that in the imagination of those who conceptualised that ad for Wendy's and of the larger society in which he lives, he is only an improved version of those native cannibals by virtue of the accident of his birth in Canada? Do you explain to an eight-year-old that in all the Great Books of this society, those cannibals are his ancestors, his kinsmen? How do you handle the fact that the word 'tribesmen', complete with all its Western baggage, has somehow crept into the vocabulary of your eight-year-old son and you didn't even realise it? That the boy from Ghana was so disgusted when he uttered the word 'tribesmen' was particularly worrisome.

'Can't you see I'm busy with our guest?' the father said. 'Go back to your room and we'll talk about this later.' The boy left, sulking.

'That's a temporary escape for you,' I told my friend. 'This boy obviously thinks himself Canadian. For now he is still too young to realise that a tree trunk may spend twenty years in the river but it will never become a crocodile. There will always be the artillery of the West's stubborn image of the Other to remind him of his savage origins. You're lucky he still doesn't realise his kinship with Wendy's cannibals.'

'Pius, it's easy for you to sermonise now,' my friend responded. 'Your daughter is only three months old. Wait until you reach this bridge. I know of no African parents here in the West who do not face this problem.'

'Has your son ever been to Ghana?' I asked my friend. He replied in the negative but told me he was making plans to take him home soon. That's part of the problem, I told him. Those of us here have two options. Our first option is to raise children who are going to be completely deluded that they are Canadians or Americans, that they are not like 'those cannibals and tribesmen', whereas the imagery of otherness and its economies of meaning will follow them their entire lives, never mind that they 'speak English with no accent'! Our second option is to raise multicultural children who have no illusions about who they really are deep down, beneath the surface of hybridity, even if their passports and their accents tell other stories, other supposed narratives of modernity.

'How do you do that when the cards are so thoroughly dealt against us?' my friend ventured. 'We don't even have the pedagogical resources to counter Wendy's narrative at age-appropriate levels. Take the case of your countryman,

Chinua Achebe. *Things Fall Apart* is great material. Do we have abridged, children's versions of that great African book? If my son had encountered masquerades in age-appropriate versions of *Things Fall Apart*, perhaps his question today would have been, "Dad, why is Wendy's making those masquerades look bad?"'

Now that was a brilliant point I hadn't even thought about. 'Well, there is always a start,' I exclaimed. 'Subscribe to Setanta Sports. Make sure your son watches the Nations Cup with you. Let him add Stephen Appiah, Samuel Eto'o, Didier Drogba, and Nwankwo Kanu to his list of sports heroes composed exclusively for now of names from Canadian ice hockey and American football and basketball!'

We laughed and returned to our football talk, but something had changed about the evening. On my way home, I thought about my three-month-old daughter. What will I tell her, how will I react when she is older, goes to school here in Canada, and returns home one day to ask me about tribesmen from Africa?

11

AFRICA, *VANITY FAIR*, AND THE VANITY OF A COVER

I know of no African who would pick up the July 2007 issue of *Vanity Fair* and not bow his or her head in anger, pent-up frustration, sadness, and helplessness. Anger flowing from the realisation that close to a century of international critical interventionism to redefine the terms of our representation has cut absolutely no ice with our historical oppressors; pent-up frustration flowing from the fact that even the most well-meaning agents in Prospero's household – those who have carved a global niche for themselves in the Mercy Industrial Complex as our 'voices', our 'representatives', 'one of us' – continue to act subconsciously from the same base and reprehensible instincts that have guided Prospero's representation of Africa for the last five hundred years; sadness that we are some two thousand years beyond the point at which we can reasonably utter the expression made famous by the carpenter son of Joseph: 'Father, forgive them for they know not what they do!'

Prospero's contemporary incarnations in the West's

Mercy Industrial Complex know what they are doing. The proof is in this cover of *Vanity Fair*. One glance at it and you immediately notice a few things that indicate bad news. The cover screams that this special issue on Africa is guest-edited by *Bono*! That's the first red flag. Bono is synonymous with a certain territory, with certain modes of representing Africa. You know immediately that you are in the territory of the Mercy Industrial Complex. No need to open the magazine. You know the territory. You know what you are going to find inside. You know the keywords of the industry: aid, HIV/AIDS, etc.

And if you think that *Vanity Fair* is going to at least wait until you open the magazine before shoving AIDS in your face, you have another think coming! After all, we talking Africa, ain't we? And so we enter the territory of HIV/AIDS, right there on the cover! 'Uganda,' we are told, 'has successfully reversed its national HIV/AIDS rate from a high of almost 18 per cent in the 1990s to less than 7 per cent today.' How moving! The position of that statement – we are not told the source of these statistics; we are just expected to swallow them! – on the cover is itself a study in aesthetic carelessness. The words are tucked between the smiling lips of an ecstatic Melinda Gates and the attentive ears of a dreamy Oprah Winfrey. Like the missionaries of yore, Melinda Gates seems to be bringing to Oprah the good tidings of the salvation of Africa, her ancestral homeland. Colonialist tropes have a way of entering into the picture at the most unexpected moments. A patriarchal Bill Gates, also staring into Africa's future, completes the picture of this curious cover.

By now your mind should be approaching the obvious question: what are three American billionaires doing on the cover of such an important magazine when the special and 'historic' issue is devoted exclusively to Africa? *Vanity Fair* is, no doubt, telling us that after sending its radar on a fishing expedition across the vast expanse of Africa, it could not find three or even a single African worthy of gracing the cover of its special Africa issue. From Nelson Mandela to Desmond Tutu, from Wole Soyinka to Chinua Achebe, from Wangari Maathai to Ngozi Okonjo-Iweala, from Cardinal Francis Arinze to Youssou N'Dour, from Samuel Eto'o Fils to Didier Drogba, from Kofi Annan to Ellen Johnson Sirleaf – no, not one! By now you know the considerations that must have gone into the making of this cover. *Vanity Fair* is in America, right there in the belly of the capitalist beast. Market and profit are the Siamese twins playing the game here.

Although putting three of the most prominent faces – and the deepest pockets – in the Mercy Industrial Complex on this cover is meant to dress the twins respectably and give them a human face, don't ever forget that the well-fed, non-diseased Africa that the face of a Wole Soyinka or a Kofi Annan represents does not and cannot sell magazines in the West. Put crudely, no combination of African faces would sell this issue of *Vanity Fair* like the three faces that were chosen in their place. It is one thing for *Vanity Fair* to serve as a platform for Bono's messianic vanity; it is another thing entirely for us to expect the decision makers at *Vanity Fair* to forget profit while trying to look good to a diseased continent whose most accomplished sons and daughters just cannot sell the magazine. After all, we are not talking France, Japan, or China. It is simply inconceivable that a special issue of *Vanity Fair* on any of these three countries would carry three American faces on its cover. This is where the inconsequential humanity of you, my African friend, comes into the picture.

But you're not done yet with this cover. You see, you're stubborn and you just can't accept that the cover has no redeeming feature. So, you fish out your reading glasses. There are some hidden texts in extremely small font. There may be something there. Ah, it's a list of global celebrities that *Vanity Fair*'s Annie Leibovitz has assembled to add to the glitz and glamour of this 'historic' issue of the magazine. You begin to scrutinise the list: Muhammad Ali, Maya Angelou, Warren Buffet, George W. Bush, Don Cheadle, George Clooney, Djimon Hounsou, Iman, Jay-Z, Alicia Keys, Madonna, Barack Obama, Brad Pitt, Queen Rania of Jordan, Condoleezza Rice, Chris Rock, Archbishop Desmond Tutu.

Ah, finally they found some space for three Africans – Hounsou, Iman, and Tutu – even if you needed a magnifying glass to detect them! Under the circumstances, this is a considerable concession on the part of *Vanity Fair* and Bono.

Then you open the magazine and discover that more Conradian horror awaits you. And you thought the cover could not be surpassed in its thoughtlessness! You discover that this Africa issue is actually a safari that starts from – wait for it! – the Diplomatic Reception Room at the White House! I am willing to wager here, again, that a special issue on France would have started at the Élysée. We are treated to the set of the cover shoot of George Bush and Condoleeza Rice. The caption reads: 'Into Africa' via the White House! *Vanity Fair* attempts to save the day by serving you photo shoots of Cheadle, Obama, and Ali. Welcome to Africa, via its more tolerable, sanitised black diasporic face!

But *Vanity Fair* is not done yet. Right above the heads of these famous diasporic blacks is another unimaginative caption: 'The 21 people who put their famous faces to work for this issue say it all. Annie Leibovitz paired them up on 20 different covers –shout-outs for the challenge, the promise and the future of Africa.' The *challenge*, the *promise*, and the *future* of Africa? And somewhere in the minds of Bono and whoever worked with him at *Vanity Fair* to conceptualise this issue, the challenge, the promise, and the future of Africa are best represented by eighteen American faces and three African faces thrown in perfunctorily in a gesture of depraved tokenism!

12

OJU L'ORO WA!

Oju l'oro wa. The face is the abode of discourse. When and how did the Yoruba genius come up with this adage? Often, the African genius packs ancestral wisdoms and an entire world into just one saying. If you are the type that constantly tries to listen to the wisdoms of your cultural matrix, you encounter them constantly in glittering nuggets as the business we call living takes you around on its quotidian grind. If you are outside of your cultural world, if Euro-America is where your head has led your feet in the quest for your daily bread, every encounter with the enduring verities of your people's proverbs becomes an occasion for critical reflection. It is even better if those living out such verities of your culture, wittingly or unwittingly, are Euro-Americans. You remember quietly that only a couple of decades ago, these people dismissed such sayings as foolish and childish, the products of primitive and pre-logical minds.

I'm in Ottawa. I stand in line behind her at the bank. She is a stereotype here in the Western world. She is anywhere in her mid-seventies to the advanced nineties. She is bent and wrinkled, uses a cane, and wears thick-rimmed glasses. Whenever I see her, my mind pictures the proverbial dry bones in *Things Fall Apart*. She can be quick to anger and very easily irritated, her temper not helped by the insidious but devastating ageism of her culture. Never mind those signs in the bus and other public spaces that implore you to give way and room to seniors. Those are the politically correct and hypocritical veneers worn by a deeply ageist civilisation. Scratch that surface and the bitter truth becomes evident: her type is not to be revered as a repository of knowledge. Her culture considers her an eyesore, to be packed off to an old people's home where, if the situation demands, she could be made to wear a diaper.

If she is lucky, she gets the occasional visit from her child/children. If she is unlucky, she gets the occasional postcard. Sometimes, she escapes this fate, lives alone in an apartment in town, and runs her errands once a week, always at the same places – the bank, post office, grocery store, dentist, family doctor, and vet doctor – all errands that would be run for her by doting children, grandchildren, sons- and daughters-in-law, and the entire town in my own part of the world. You pray quietly not to be behind her in traffic, as she is likely to be doing twenty miles an hour where the limit is eighty. You pray not to be stuck behind her in the queue at the bank or post office. Political correctness requires that you do not say these things. The West prefers polite, quiet, and civilised ageism. Hence, you notice that if she is first in the queue, the younger, more productive segments of society for whom time is money quietly disappear. They will come back later.

You see, you can't really blame them. This old lady has time on her hands. Unlike the young, her best days are behind her. She is not hurrying. She cannot afford to hurry. Hurrying only inches her closer to that final destination every human is reluctant to reach. So once she gets to the teller, she throws in a conversation about every mundane issue in the world while endorsing checks, paying bills, and reviewing her account. Her cat is misbehaving. Her dog was at the vet's yesterday. Speaking of which, she is thinking of changing vets. Dr Woodstone is no longer what he used to be. The weather has been crazy lately, eh? Developers are putting up another high-rise in her neighbourhood. What's the world coming to? The queue builds up behind her ...

Then she's finally done. As she turns to leave, the polite teller adds: 'Ma'm, have you considered Internet banking? You could do these things from the comfort of your own home, you know?' She smiles and I curse the teller quietly. He's now opened up space for another hour of mundane conversation! She turns back to the teller and says, 'Sure. I've tried to do my banking online but I just don't like it. Maybe it's me, but I prefer to see the face of the person who takes care of my money. I can't help it. I prefer to see your face as we review my finances. Internet banking doesn't let me do that.' By now, I'm no longer glancing at my wristwatch every second. I'm no longer irritated. I've logged into that automatic part of my cerebral software that is always processing every detail to determine their value for cultural scholarship.

I prefer to see your face ... The Internet doesn't let me do that. I look around me. I'm the only non-Caucasian in the room. In essence, the teller and all the customers heard: 'I prefer to see your face.' It doesn't go deeper than that for them. I'm the only one who heard differently. She spoke English, I heard Yoruba. She said: I prefer to see your face. I heard: *Oju l'oro wa* (The face is the abode of discourse). Unknown to everyone in that banking hall, an entire ideoscape of cultural significations had jumped into the elderly woman's conversation with the teller and I was processing it in situ. I was reaching out to the old woman from an entirely different universe of discourse. I was tempted to tell her that her preference for the face of the teller, the flicks of the eyelids, the twitch of every muscle, the creases of the brow, the smiles, the frowns, and the dance of the lips are all crucial to the morphology of human contact in my own part of the world where communication is communion and communal.

I was tempted to tell her that there is a bitter irony in the fact she is fighting a battle against the intrusions of too much technology while in my own part of the world we are losing the war against the dehumanisation and depersonalisation of discourse. It has become well-nigh impossible to insist on ways of being underwritten by that Yoruba philosophy *oju l'oro wa*, when we all now live in the civilisation of impersonal propinquity that defines the MAC (mutually assured connectivity) age. Within a single decade, I have watched as MAC invaded the theatres of my interactions with my immediate and extensive extended family back home, transforming what used to be psychically empowering human contact into perfunctory phatic interaction.

We moved from the family insisting that I come home at least once a year to their insisting on regular cellphone conversation. These days, my army of undergraduate nephews and nieces are no longer insisting on any of those forms of contact. They make the cellphone feel really passé. Now, it's all Facebook, MySpace, Twitter, and Hi5. They expect me to spend a few hours every day chatting with them in virtual space. Five or ten years ago, it was: 'Uncle, when are you coming home? We want to see you.' Now, nobody is asking to see me anymore. They are content with asking me to sign into Facebook and sending me stuff like: 'LOL! Uncle, thanx 4 d pics. Really 9ice. Saw ur mom 2day. OMG! She looks good 4 her age. Yes, I saw it too. LMAO!' In essence, it's not just difficult to create a space of valuation for *oju l'oro wa* in this new universe of discourse; one's vocabulary must also begin to resemble ancient Chinese calligraphy. Everything is shorthand and fast-foodish. When my ignorance of the vocabulary of virtual communication was threatening to cut me off from half my family back in Nigeria, I had to declare a personal state of emergency. I went online to look for a glossary of virtual space communication. There I saw things like LOL = Laugh out loud; OMG = Oh my God; LMAO = Laughing my ass off; etc.

When I joked about all this with my mom, she laughed and told me that things have gotten to a stage where some of those nieces and nephews spend weeks in the same town – they are mostly in universities in Ilorin, Ibadan, and Zaria – without seeing one another. Apparently, one of my nieces had phoned my mom and when asked if she'd delivered a message to another niece in the same school, she told my mom that they hadn't seen each other in a while but they chat every day on Facebook. And yes, she delivered my mom's message to her on Facebook! Both nieces are undergraduate students of Ahmadu Bello University. I imagine them in different cybercafes on opposite ends of campus or each in her hostel bedroom with a Blackberry. It's now too much of an effort to meet up at a cafeteria and do *oju l'oro wa*.

In the midst of all this despair about the fate, space, and place of the human in the MAC age, an age that is beginning to look like a dangerously literal version of Francis Fukuyama's 'post-human' age, an old Caucasian woman insists on *oju l'oro wa* in a bank in faraway Canada! Africa has a way of winning little battles in the arena of meaning.

PART THREE

DIALOGUES AND DISSENSIONS

13

I, SARAH BAARTMAN, INVISIBLE!

Dear Sandra and Susan,

I salute you both in the name of feminism, women's liberation, gender equality, and, most importantly, global sisterhood. The publication of your much-anticipated *Feminist Literary Theory and Criticism: A Norton Reader* is such an epochal event that I must interrupt the blissful and well-deserved eternal sleep that was eventually accorded me when the people and government of France, ever so fatherly and motherly when it comes to taking care of poor Africa, graciously returned my brain and backside to the South African government for burial in my ancestral homeland a few years ago. I join the American and the global feminist family in congratulating the two of you on the publication of this truly wonderful volume. It is obvious that feminist intellectual labour will never ever be the same again. Resounding success, I must say, has become synonymous with the long history of intellectual collaboration between the two of you. After all, *The Mad Woman in the Attic*, the first gift of your collaborative efforts to humanity, has remained the only unavoidable bible of feminist scholarship ever since it was published.

The reference to the magnanimity of France in returning my remains to the government and people of South Africa should have given away my identity by now. However, it is always safer and wiser to swear by the natural invisibility of Africa and Africans in matters of global import. And in your immediate context in the United States, it is outright foolish to assume that anybody considers anything about Africa worth knowing. Except, of course, hunger, starvation, poverty, wars, AIDS, famine, and Western charity or 'giving' (apologies to former president Bill Clinton). I must therefore assume complete ignorance of my identity and introduce myself. I hope you will find it in your hearts to pardon my presumptuousness if you are both already familiar with my story.

My name is Sarah Baartman, also famously known internationally as the 'Hottentot Venus'. I will spare you the sassy details of my story and focus only on the essential. In 1810 I was lured to London, where I soon became a prisoner of Europe's rapacious and capitalistic voyeurism. I'm sure I don't have to tell you the story of nineteenth-century Europe and its treatment of its Others in Africa and other places. No doubt you still remember your *orientalism* – Edward Said has been a very good friend since he got here. The Europe of this period was also a formidable theatre of all kinds of exhibitions. Zoophilism was in the air. The coloured Other needed to be displayed publicly and regularly in London, Paris, and Lisbon as colonial fauna. As fate always manages to arrange these things, I was what Europeans called – and still call – an 'African tribeswoman' gifted with an exceptional backside. Europe's science promptly concluded that my buttocks suffered from a biological deformity known as steatopygia. The lips of my womanhood were also considered to be too huge and elongated for the civilised global standards determined by the labia of white women. And so from Britain to France my backside and the lips of my womanhood became objects of visual consumption in the public spheres of white patriarchy. For an extra fee, white men could even touch my behind while I was on display.

Death eventually came calling. You must know that where I come from in Africa, death is no finality. I merely transitioned to ancestorhood in the world view of my people, hence the reverence with which Africans treat the dead. Not so Europeans. They took their knives and carving objects; carved out my brain, the lips of my womanhood, and my backside; put them in bottles; and kept them in public display at the Musée de l'Homme in Paris. Yes, I can see you cringe. You should. All sensitive feminists should. The idea, just the idea! The bitter tragedy of a woman's most vital parts captured by men, carved out of her dead body by men, and stored in the Museum of Man! Of all places! My parts remained in public view in that museum, ultimate evidence of patriarchy's victory over feminism, until 1974, when they were withdrawn into a private sanctuary. Finally, in 2002, France returned her precious conquest to the people of South Africa.

Dear sisters, the significance of my story to the feminist cause and to global feminist intellectual labour should be quite obvious by now. For nearly two centuries, I was an international feminist cause célèbre, the very embodiment of patriarchal control over African female sexuality, black female sexuality, and, I daresay, female sexuality. Let me be clear: the story of my body in the international economy of meaning is the story of your own bodies, the story of every woman's body. The difference lies merely in the detail, or what your postmodernist colleagues would call 'local particularities'.

Given the fact that my narrative has become one of the most formidable sites – I hate it when I sound like you academics! – of global feminist contestation and intellection, it stands to reason that any rational person would expect me to make a grand, celebrated entrance into your Norton volume through the work of any of the numerous African feminist scholars of international repute who have written about me. At the risk of sounding immodest, nobody would expect to pick up a summation of five centuries of feminist intellectual labour – which your Norton anthology represents – and draw a blank with regard to the story of Sarah Baartman. After all, I've been theorised, postcolonised, and postmodernised in all the faddish versions of feminisms out there. I didn't think it was possible for me to be disappeared in any serious historiographical account of feminist theory. I didn't expect to be Ralph Ellisoned.

Trust me, my dear sisters, I was not motivated to write you by any narcissistic self-indulgence. You will admit, from what you now know of my story, that I am quite used to being silenced, being disappeared. I am actually more worried by the broader, deeper ideological implications of your having softly disappeared me from your Norton volume. I am interested in the stories told – or untold – by your editorial choices and options, the instinct to include and the impulse to exclude. I am interested in the conscious and subconscious processes that led you to the conclusion that Africa, a huge continent of fifty-four countries and over a billion people, has contributed nothing, absolutely nothing, to five centuries of feminist theorising. After all, as seasoned academics in the United States, you both know that exclusions tell much louder stories than inclusions. I know we are on the same page here.

Some people may praise you for making this volume truly global and representative by including the multilayered voices of the Other. They would be right if they did that. After all, you included essays by bell hooks, Hortense Spillers, Alice Walker, Toni Morrison, and Audre Lorde, evidence of your awareness of Africana feminist voices and practices; you included essays by Gayatri Spivak and Chandra Mohanty, evidence of your awareness of the expansive field of Third World/postcolonial/ transnational feminist voices and practices; the entry by Paula Gunn Allen saved the day for Native American feminisms; Gloria Anzaldúa – another good friend of mine here – thankfully guarantees the presence of Chicana feminisms in your volume. In essence, the presence of these Other voices, strategically sprinkled in the text, is a laudable proof of the fact that you paid attention when Hazel Carby screamed in an article, 'White Woman Listen!' You listened. You agreed with her that feminism could and should no longer be the gospel of the white Western female according to Betty Friedan, Germaine Greer, Gloria Steinem, Kate Millett, Judith Butler, Diana Fuss, Elaine Showalter, and others too numerous to mention. You agreed with Carby that the narratives of the French delegation – Simone de Beauvoir, Luce Irigaray, Hélène Cixous, Monique Wittig, and Julia Kristeva – should no longer be deemed universal. You agreed that Chinese women are probably better positioned to speak for and about themselves than to be represented and spoken for by Julia Kristeva's *About Chinese Women*.

It is your awareness of these things that makes your excision of African feminist theories and theorists from your volume all the more alarming. Could it be that you imagined that the voices of the African American women you selected adequately speak for those of their continental sisters? Possibly. If this is the case, I must tell you that African American women cannot be made to stand in and speak for continental African women. According to an African proverb, the monkey and the gorilla may claim oneness, but monkey is monkey and gorilla gorilla. Perhaps you imagined that African women would be better served if granted some space beneath the Third World/postcolonial/ transnational feminist umbrella you represented with the voices of Gayatri Spivak and Chandra Mohanty? Possibly. Could it be that you are simply unaware of the considerable body of African feminist intellection right there in your neck of the woods in the

US academy? Possibly. Could it be that you just simply elected to disappear them like you disappeared me? Possibly.

I'm sure you know that Bill O'Reilly, the famous talkative right-wing fundamentalist on Fox News, has only just discovered in 2007 that African Americans are capable of eating properly with fork and knife – you know, like real, normal people. I don't want you to travel that path. I don't want you to discover, only now, that continental African women have been theorising feminism for a very long time in US academe and have produced a considerable body of work, one or two pieces of which should deservedly have passed through the eye of Norton's needle. Since you included work by Alice Walker, I take it that you both know how well her theory of 'womanism' has travelled in US and global women's studies programmes and departments. The trouble is, in 1985, before Walker used the term, Chikwenye Okonjo Ogunyemi, a US-based Nigerian feminist scholar, had published an essay in *Signs* entitled 'Womanism: The Dynamics of the Contemporary Black Female Novel in English'. Now *Signs* is not a journal the two of you could have missed. It's the most prestigious peer-reviewed journal of feminist studies in the United States. But let's assume you somehow missed that issue. Ogunyemi subsequently published a very important book, *Africa Wo/Man Palava*, with the University of Chicago Press in 1996. Did you also miss that? We're talking U of Chicago Press, for God's sake!

There is also Obioma Nnaemeka, a formidable feminist theorist based at Indiana University. Her reputation is global. Secure. Frankly speaking, her essay 'Feminism, Rebellious Women, and Cultural Boundaries' has no business not making your Norton Reader. There is, of course, her formidable work on female circumcision in Africa. By the way, isn't female circumcision in Africa – genital mutilation in Western parlance – supposed to be a subject of sensational predilection for Western feminists and NGOs? If not a single excerpt from

Obioma Nnaemeka's *Female Circumcision and the Politics of Knowledge: African Women in Imperialist Discourses* made it into your volume, don't you think that something is awfully wrong? There is also Oyeronke Oyewumi, another important US-based feminist theorist. The University of Minnesota Press published her book, *The Invention of Women: Making an African Sense of Western Gender Discourses*, to critical acclaim in 1997. Not even a chapter from this book is worthy of inclusion? There is also Ifi Amadiume. She teaches at Dartmouth. Her *Male Daughters, Female Husbands: Gender and Sex in an African Society* is a priceless classic. Did you also miss that? There are Molara Ogundipe and Nkiru Nzegwu. How about the Egyptian Nawal El Saadawi and the Algerian Assia Djebar? These two global figures of women's writing and feminist intellectual labour have written nothing that could have made the cut and rescued an entire continent? You will notice that I have refrained from mentioning any of the numerous important feminist thinkers based in Africa. I do not want to bore you. It seems better to cite those whose alterity in US academe one would have believed you couldn't conceivably have missed.

I read sadly in your preface that 'our own conversations about the construction of this book have been enhanced by many colleagues and friends who have shared syllabi with us, discussed their teaching practices, and made suggestions about possible inclusions'. A long list of names follows and this is where the sadness lies: that not once in all these conversations with this expansive cast of consultants did my story and the story of Africa's contribution to feminist theorising crop up. Not one person, not one colleague across the feminist studies landscape in the US pointed out this ominous oversight – if indeed it was an oversight – to you? Obioma Nnaemeka is Susan Gubar's neighbour in Indiana, for Christ's sake!

There is some good news, however. There won't be a shortage of happy African intellectuals who will query the wisdom of even expecting Africa to have been included in your work in the first place. Why do we always whine and complain when Westerners ignore us? they will say. It is not their responsibility to include us. We should include ourselves by creating our own structures, period! After all, Oyeronke Oyewumi, as if anticipating what would happen with your Norton project, had edited *African Gender Studies: A Reader* in 2005. Such opinions would, of course, ignore the simple fact that your work has a universalising underpinning in terms of its historical breadth and thematic scope and Africa has been excluded from this picture. They would ignore the fact that this is Norton and who says Norton says canons! They would ignore the fact that even if we were to adopt the reductionist approach that all you have done here is to reflect the multiple voices that have inflected feminist, gender, and women studies in the American academy over the years, the end product conveys the fallacious message that no African woman has been part of this process.

I know you are already wondering how an African woman, who died so many years ago with no evidence of having attended any university, happens to be so familiar with academic language and procedure. You should know the answer to that: I'm now an ancestor, a spirit. I'm not human. I'm supposed to know everything. That is what sanctions my intervention in the affairs of you mortals!

Peace and love,
Sarah Baartman

14

LETTER TO AN OLD FLAME

Dear Africa,

Greetings from Australia! Well, how time flies! It's the ninth anniversary of our divorce and I thought I should seize the occasion to write and find out how you're doing. Strictly for old times' sake, since we have both moved on with our lives. I must apologise again for my letter that leaked in the year 2000 and caused both of us so much embarrassment. I know you never believed me, but I must tell you again that I never meant to make it public. We had just divorced, emotions were still raw, and I felt an urgent need to write down why I gave up on you, Africa. It was a note to myself. How it got to the Internet and circulated so widely, I will never know. The accursed Internet is also the reason why I'm unable to ever be completely sealed off from all the information going around about you. I try, but the Internet won't let me get away from you. Perhaps it's the same with you? Do you still think about me sometimes? I know the answer. Africa, you are what Nigerians call the Oyingbo market. You don't miss any absent market woman.

Perhaps I am wrong to call you an old flame? Perhaps our love story still hasn't ended? After all, you took up some three decades of my life before I realised that you were always going to hold my white skin and my history against me despite my love for you. No matter how much I laboured in African studies, that field of knowledge that assembles your children, lovers, admirers, friends, foes, and all who desire to know you and build up a knowledge storehouse about you for future generations, I was always going to be the *mzungu*, the white man whose ancestors did terrible things to you and whose contemporaries in Washington, London, and Paris continue to do terrible things to you. I was permanently guilty by association and heritage.

Even when I noticed that some of your so-called autochthonous children were capable of inflicting such injuries on you and themselves that would make Adolf Hitler recoil in humane indignation, you insisted that the explanation must be found outside, somehow tied to what my ancestors did to you. Intra- and inter-ethnic clashes in East Africa? I was responsible. Islamic militants in northern Nigeria transforming the periodic slaughter of Igbo people into the sixth pillar of their own brand of Islam? I was responsible. Africa's political elite would rather shore up their personal and class fortunes than develop their people and their countries? I was responsible. Cholera outbreak in Zimbabwe? I was responsible. The slaughter of child-witches by Christians in southern Nigeria? I was responsible. Name it, I was responsible. My white skin became a feel-good, psychological salve needed to rationalise the monumental demission of your own children.

Now this was quite depressing. Trust me, I would have trudged on had my own academic labours translated to even the minutest, verifiable result in terms of ameliorating your piteous and visibly worsening condition. But nothing worked. I tried theory. It didn't work. I tried praxis. It didn't work. And, of course, my original sin of being a white Africanist pretending to have any answers was always going to stand in the way. So, I 'checked out' of African studies like Nigeria's famous 'Andrew'. Now what is this I hear that you have now turned the relentless nativism with which you put me out of business against your own children? What is this I hear about a fundamentalist nativism that has a worrisomely increasing number of your children transform location in Africa into a precondition for validity and authenticity in African studies? What is this I hear about a new politics of exclusion that is busy linking location in Africa with morality and ethics, thereby criminalising the trajectories and choices of your children who have opted to write Africa from Euro-American locations?

The stories I hear from this part of the world are sufficiently depressing. I know I shouldn't gloat but I almost feel justified that I left you. What have I not heard? Where do I start? Many are the stories of your children in Euro-America who return home for periodic engagements with continental communities of discourse and find themselves in tricky territory. They walk on thorns and nails, constantly having to contend with sly and not-so-sly delegitimations of whatever it is they have to say and offer. From the hostile 'Who the heck do you think you are?' or 'What do you know about these things?' to the patronising 'You know, things have changed since you left', from the accusatory 'If we all left like you ...' to the irritating 'You now think and act like them' and the dismissive 'Is it because you are abroad?', the underlying message is never ambiguous: *You may still be us, but you are no longer sufficiently us*. The quality of their Africanness has been diluted, forever suspect.

This explains why your children plying their trade in the white man's land exhibit dangerous symptoms of what I call the Okonkwo complex. If Okonkwo of *Things Fall Apart* lived in a visceral fear of being deemed effeminate, your children abroad live in permanent fear of being deemed uppity and arrogant by the sentinels of authenticity and legitimacy back home. The symptoms of their Okonkwo complex are easy to recognise when they are attending academic events back home and communing with 'home colleagues' who must certify them 'still somewhat us' at the end of the exercise. The exaggerated display of affability, the excessive use of local lingo, the continuous performance of humility, the hesitation and gruesome mental calculations before paying for the beer in social gatherings – pay too quickly and you could be guilty of assuming that colleagues at home are paupers, don't pay quickly enough and you could be guilty of being stingy despite your dollars and euros. It's a lose-lose situation for these diasporic Okonkwos. Every statement, every sentence is susceptible to misinterpretation: 'Are you trying to say that those of us at home are not brilliant, not the very best in our fields?' I need not get into how each of the roving children manages the variations of this scenario they experience when they go home. They all have and know their own stories.

It is the *mission moralisatrice* of the new attitudes of nativism and authenticity emanating from your home-based children that is so invidious and so utterly counterproductive. The divergent and extremely rich transnational trajectories of your children working in Euro-America are simply lumped into a monolithic basket of flight, treachery, and abandonment. Movement becomes at once immoral and amoral. It has even gotten to a point where some of your children who used to be outside but who have returned to Africa join the morality dance as soon as they get home. They begin to author essays that frame their return narratives as acts of moral courage, which leave no one in doubt that they are really indicting those 'amoral' colleagues abroad who have not followed their example by returning to the proverbial African classroom.

Like all totalistic discourses, the discourse of nativistic morality assumes that the African classroom is a concept that is easily defined and need not be problematised. What is an

African classroom? When is a classroom African? I know of one of your children who teaches in Canada. Last semester, he had ninety-five undergraduates in his AFRI 1001 (Introduction to African Studies) course. Sixty-six of those students were from Africa. Not Africans born in Canada. They were from Africa. They were from thirty-two of Africa's fifty-four countries. Yes, one of your amoral children who abandoned African classrooms had thirty-two African countries assembled in just one undergraduate class in Canada. He taught more than half the continent in one course. What are the chances of having this sort of geographic swathe in a single classroom in such 'authentic sites' as Ibadan, Legon, or Makerere? Is an African studies class with sixty-six students from thirty-two African countries an African classroom? Is a classroom in Tunis with sixty-six Arab students who are plugged into their psychic and cultural affiliations with the Middle East an African classroom? Is a classroom in Stellenbosch with sixty-six Afrikaner students who belong heart and soul to their European imaginaries and are overly conscious of their First World circumstances an African classroom? Again, when is a classroom African?

Africa, if, like a Molue or Matatu bus driver, you continue on this slope towards an exclusivist, nombrilistic nativism, I fear you may end up insisting that mucus-nosed and underdressed African students must be gathered in the open (under dogon yaro trees) and taught by volunteers from international charitable organisations, using chalk and other pedagogical materials donated by UNICEF, before you are satisfied that the stringent and sacrosanct requirements of an 'authentic African classroom' have been met.

In essence, anyone not holding evening graduate seminars in overcrowded classrooms illuminated by paraffin lamps must be deemed to have made the amoral choice of abandoning the African classroom. Anyone not using stencil and Gestetner machines to roll out exam question papers in the twenty-first century has abandoned ship. At this rate, you may even insist on reviewing the case of Nigerian faculty in Ghanaian universities in order to determine if they are guilty of abandoning the African classroom. After all, they left the terrible conditions of Nigerian classrooms for the slightly more infrastructurally auspicious conditions of Ghanaian classrooms.

I have so many other things to say but this letter has already gotten so long. I am not even sure you won't be offended by my frank observations. I am not certain I still have the right to dabble into your affairs after our divorce. What do I even know? I am just an old white man now teaching international development studies in Australia. I loved you. I still do.

Your old flame

15

AN EX-AFRICAN WRITES TO PRESIDENT SARKOZY

Dear President Sarkozy,

Please allow me to introduce myself to you. I am an ex-African, or a former African. I now consider myself more French than the French. When I was an African, I was a patriot who hated the uses to which the civilisation of France was put in places like Indochina, Algeria, Madagascar, and so many places where the people of France displayed unsurpassable brutality. I hated the France that participated in slavery, the France that colonised, the France that civilised, the France that tortured, the hypocritical France that still despises 'le black' and 'le beur' while parading Thierry Henry and Zinedine Zidane as its finest gifts to humanity in recent times.

I hated this France until very recently. Now I've seen the light! Like Doc Gynéco, I've fallen in love with the France of Jean-Marie Le Pen, the France of Charles Pasqua, the France of you, my brother, Nicolas Sarkozy. I take back every negative thing I've said, written, or thought about my beloved France. Those were my days of ignorance. *Mea culpa, mea maxima culpa*! I have now washed myself clean of the blight of my uncivilised African origins. I no longer have any trace of the jungle left in me. I sleep and dream every day of my brand-new ancestors the Gauls. And as you know, I do not just speak French; I speak *le Français de France*, *le Français du Français*, *le Français français*, just like brother Léon Damas of Guyana. You and I can now speak of our common heritage, our common history, our culture, and our civilisation.

On the basis of our new and unimpeachable bond, I want to commend you for the valiant efforts you made to ensure that our compatriots who were recently found guilty of child kidnapping and trafficking in Chad were returned to us to serve their prison terms in Paris. It beats me that those uncivilised Africans would actually imagine that we would allow French criminals to serve jail time in Africa! In N'Djamena of all places! Unimaginable. Isn't it insulting enough that dignified French criminals had to suffer the indignity of passing through an African judicial system and be treated like ordinary African criminals to boot? Imagine the emotional and psychological toll this treatment must have taken. I hope you will put pressure on the Chadian president to consider paying compensation to our criminals.

Really, these are times when I regret that we still haven't found a proper replacement for my brother, the great Jacques Foccart. There just will never be another *Monsieur Afrique* like him. He was a great man. He knew his Africa; he knew his Africans. They were like his children. When Jacques Foccart handled Africa on behalf of *La République*, Africans were very well-behaved children. Things would never have degenerated to a point where a *Président de la République* personally had to travel to Chad to secure the release of our criminals. One phone call from Foccart and Chadian President Idriss Déby would have pissed in his pants. For more than three decades, Foccart raised and nurtured the boys who served us so well: Étienne Gnassingbé Eyadéma, Abdou Diouf, Paul Biya, Omar Bongo, Félix Houphouët-Boigny, Mathieu Kérékou, Denis Sassou Nguesso, Modibo Kéita, and so many others. Even Mobutu Sese Seko, who belonged to the Belgians, knew that his bread was buttered only when he recognised Foccart's authority. Every family has a black sheep. Our black sheep in those days was Thomas Sankara, who consistently misbehaved and reared his vegetable head on our path. Foccart arranged for him to be disciplined by Blaise Compaoré ...

This brings me to my next point. In less than one year of your presidency, you've visited Gabon, Senegal, Chad, and a few other places in Africa. In Senegal you gave that great speech, but Africans have reacted to it with characteristic ingratitude. No surprise here. They were never grateful for the civilisation we took to them anyway. My point, however, is that you're fraternising too much and too frequently with Africans. It is one thing for us to make them happy by calling them partners in the *Francophonie*; it is another matter entirely if your behaviour begins to create the erroneous impression that the said partnership is, for us, anything more than the productive partnership between a horse and its rider. We must never forget that they are still subjects of our vast neocolony. Familiarity breeds contempt. We already have unpalatable consequences of your trips to Africa on our laps ...

You have spent almost two precious decades of your public career waging a jihad against the immoral and amoral effects of black and Arab presence in our clean, pure, and intrinsically moral Aryan cities in France. You and I agree that every single problem of moral decadence and degeneracy one encounters in Paris, for instance, is attributable to the presence of those undesirable, hungry *racaille* (scum) from West Africa and the Maghreb. Just look at what they have turned neighbourhoods like Barbès and Belleville into! These *racaille* are dirty, do not speak French, grow Islamic beards, wear Islamic foulard, marry too many wives, have too many concubines or *'deuxieme bureau'*, have too many children who drain our *sécurité sociale*. I'm not going to talk about your predecessor, Jacques Chirac, who complained, justifiably, about the 'noise and odour' of these unwanted folks who invade our dear France.

Of these undesirable attributes, polygamy, concubinage, and marital infidelity are the most alien to our pure, Christian, civilised Western white culture. They are the most formidable indices of the primordial immorality of these African people. This explains why your jihad against African and Arab immigrants has consisted in trying to demonstrate that they are just too steeped in their immoral and amoral cultures to be able to integrate fully into our civilised society. How does one expect a Malian or an Algerian not to have a harem of wives that makes a single family look like a football team? It's their culture, not ours. How does one expect a Gabonese or a Togolese, who pretends to have only one wife, not to have a string of concubines scattered all over Paris? It's their culture, not ours. How does one expect them not to cheat and lie? It's their nature, not ours. The sacrosanct essence of marital vows, so fundamental in our culture, is completely alien to Africans and Arabs.

Given these incontrovertible facts, I've been trying to understand recent developments in your own life that are completely at odds with our culture. I am not talking about the much-publicised divorce between you and Cécilia. Divorce is the Siamese twin of marriage in our Western societies. The problem I have is with the timeline of events. The mathematics is not working. No matter how one cuts it, slices it, spins it, the inevitable scenario is that you were seeing Carla Bruni – that stunning Italian model – long before you divorced Cécilia. Now that looks an awful lot like you were cheating on Cécilia, your former wife, and lying to her. That looks an awful lot like you had a girlfriend or a concubine or a '*deuxieme bureau*'.

At some point in this timeline, you had a loose form of polygamy going on. Yet you have spent an entire career explaining to the world that such behaviour – the very idea of polygamy, concubinage, '*deuxieme bureau*', marital infidelity, etc. – is alien to our pure Aryan culture and can be found only in the immoral and amoral cultures of folks from West Africa and the Maghreb. Do you see my problem now? Already, some mischievous African immigrants, who have ferociously resisted full cultural integration for a very long time, are now saying that if Sarkozy's lifestyle is emblematic of Western culture, they won't mind integrating at all! It seems to me that you are degrading our culture by making it look like the culture of Africans.

In my search for explanations, I have come up with a brilliant thesis. Since your degenerate behaviour of rotating *droits de cuissage* (conjugal duties) between Cécilia and Carla is completely alien to white culture, as you have claimed for a very long time, you must have caught the virus during your frequent trips to Africa. I think you caught what Americans call jungle fever. Definitely, Africans are to blame for your behaviour. Since you know their history so well – as your Dakar lecture reveals – you must know that the pages of our colonial library are littered with the ghosts of Europeans who ventured into the Dark Continent – the white man's grave – and were physically and metaphorically eaten up. Those who did not die lost their minds and their souls to the degeneracy of Africa. Something about the environment, the mosquitoes, the heat, the humidity, and the incomprehensible roar of jungle drums destroys the moral compass of Europeans who venture into Africa. In your own case, you went to Africa, lost the purity of our culture, and came back a lying, quasi-polygamist, two-timing ... (let's leave out the four words that would have followed in American parlance).

I am trying to start an NGO in Paris. Our aim will be to sensitise our compatriots to these things and to ensure that no future president of France will ever set foot in Africa. The risks just aren't worth the gains. This, I hope, will be my contribution to my new home, my new culture, my new society, and my new country: France!

Yours in Francophilia,
Pius Adesanmi

16

HONORARY PROSPERO: JEFF KOINANGE, CNN, AND THE MERCY INDUSTRIAL COMPLEX

CNN has unceremoniously discarded her famous Kenyan-born Africa correspondent, Jeff Koinange, like a sponge that has outlived its usefulness in the bathroom. Not surprisingly, the Internet has been awash with juicy details of the circumstances surrounding the divorce between him and his famous former employer. The cookie, it is said, crumbled for Mr Koinange owing to a combination of circumstances.

First are the embarrassing revelations of an adulterous relationship between him and Marianne Briner, a European lady with considerable connections to Kenya, who has since regaled the expansive audience of her blog with salacious and prolific details of Mr Koinange's appetite for online sexual romps, the high point of which was a catastrophic date rape in London. The trope of a successful black male crashing due to an insatiable sexual appetite for a white female has not been lost on Miss Briner's African audience, going by some of the vicious comments her blog has attracted.

Second is the fallout from Mr Koinange's most (in-)famous story about the ongoing war against a predatory Nigerian government and her international capitalist masters by freedom fighters in the Niger Delta. In the ongoing whirl of bombings, killings, and hostage taking by the Movement for the Emancipation of the Niger Delta (MEND) and other revolutionary groups determined to put an end to the environmental terrorism spearheaded by Shell and other Western oil conglomerates operating in the region, Mr Koinange visited the lion's den and did a story that had all the trappings of a James Bond movie.

Expectedly, CNN went to town with the story, broadcasting it to the point of iterative superfluity. From AC360° to American Morning, from Breaking News to Just In, from Lou Dobbs Tonight to Paula Zahn Now, CNN's audience was treated for almost an entire week to what has become a pattern of repeating one news item again and again as if on a maniacal mission to bore the audience to death. The desire here was, of course, to mine this 'dangerous' adventure into the 'heart of darkness' to CNN's maximum advantage. An ignorant Anderson Cooper actually used that racist Conradian trope in his introduction to one of his boring reruns of the story. CNN's and Mr Koinange's intentions were unmistakable. Roll tape: Anderson Cooper or Paula Zahn or John Roberts sets the tone of the story in very Conradian, very Western, characteristically ignorant terms. Audience, you are warned! We are approaching the heart of darkness! We are approaching Africa. The images you are about to see may be disturbing or outright dangerous, blah blah blah. Enter Mr Koinange – an ostensible modern-day Marlowe – in a speedboat, racing to meet the freedom fighters – or rebels/terrorists in the official-speak of the Nigerian government and the 'international community'. Suddenly, a boatload of hooded, heavily armed rebels appears from nowhere. The narrative leaves us in no doubt that Mr Koinange is in grave danger. But he is ready to lay down his life for the story, for service, for the good of humanity. Somehow, he wins the confidence of the rebels, who take him to their lair and treat him to scoops 'never before seen'. He is even allowed to film some Western hostages. Bravo, CNN!

Then the bubble burst. The Nigerian government cries foul. Mr Koinange, it would seem, had bribed everybody and everything in sight to stage his story. Expectedly, CNN insisted on the veracity of its story and the catholicity of its intentions. It was CNN's word against the Nigerian government's. And who would the international community believe – an international media behemoth like CNN or a notoriously corrupt African government? The tag 'Nigerian' didn't help matters. Enter Marianne Briner and her blog! Apart from the sex scandal, we read Mr Koinange – in his own very words – affirming to his lover that he had to do some bribing here and there to get the Niger Delta story! But who doesn't have to bribe, especially when dealing with Nigeria? A thoroughly embarrassed CNN fired him.

These are only the immediate causes of the fall of Mr Koinange. The bigger picture is where the real juice lies and that is what we must essay to dissect. Mr Koinange was bound to fall not because as a famous son of Africa with a healthy libido, opportunistic daughters of Eve were bound, sooner or later, to give him what in Nigerian parlance is called the 'PhD' (Pull Him Down) treatment; not because in the prebendal, clientilist context of operating in Africa, the dynamics of an informal economy necessitate a recourse to bribery, patronage, and other methods of getting things done and, being part of that process, Mr Koinange was bound to eventually run afoul of international standards.

In my opinion, Mr Koinange fell because of the role he assigned himself as an African in the international politics of identity which continually pitches the West against its historically constituted Others. The real world is still very much ordered along lines defined by the binary of the West and the rest, never mind the soporific, glossy, and politically correct language of globalisation, multiculturalism, integration, and other academic delusions. What has increased is the ability of people to choose and define where they belong. Mr Koinange elected to be an honorary Prospero. Not known for his/her ability to learn from history, the honorary Prospero is a persona always riding on the back of the tiger. Always, s/he ends up in the tiger's stomach in an unending Sisyphean repetition.

In the historical mission of dehumanising the Other, the real Prospero (the West) could do his own dirty work as long as he answered to names like slaver and coloniser. Although the mission has remained the same in the last five hundred or so years, Prospero no longer answers to those names. Context has changed and Prospero now answers to such names as the White House, 10 Downing Street, Bretton Woods, International Community, Transnational and Multinational Corporation, International Media, G8, Freedom (as defined by Washington), Democracy (as defined by Washington), the Security Council, the Market, Wall Street, and so many other names working for the same end: the exploitation and dehumanisation of the rest of us.

In this equation, Prospero no longer needs to personally attend to the daily task of putting down the Other. The gullible African, Arab, or Indian could be persuaded to wear a Savile Row suit, given incredible opportunities for self-advancement in Washington or London, granted citizenship and a passport. The rest is easy. This character will complete the picture by convincing himself/herself that s/he has become Prospero and will, wittingly or unwittingly, begin to do Prospero's dirty work with missionary zeal.

Anyone who has followed the 'conservative' public punditry careers of Fareed Zakaria and Dinesh D'Souza in America will understand the tragic nature of the functions of the honorary Prospero. These two were born in Bombay, but the zeal with which they now speak of 'our mission in Iraq' and 'our men and women in uniform' would make anyone believe that they were more American than Donald Rumsfeld, Dick Cheney, and Scooter Libby rolled into one. The Americanness that these two Indians perform is no surprise: the honorary Prospero must always struggle to out-Prospero Prospero.

These are the dynamics governing Mr Koinange's saga at CNN. This is how to explain how a full-blooded Kenyan criss-crossed Africa as Christopher Marlowe. I am not in any doubt that Mr Koinange genuinely believed he was serving the cause of Africa, drawing attention to the continent's benumbing tragedies. And he worked assiduously, from Sierra Leone to Liberia, from Darfur to Uganda, from the two Congos to Ethiopia, from Eritrea to the Republic of Niger! Mr Koinange brought CNN's Western audience their required daily dosage of Africa's tableau of hunger, poverty, misery, war, famine, disease, rape, and exploitation of children. Mr Koinange did well by seeking to draw global attention to these issues of conscience.

But this is where innocence stops and the ideological framing of the honorary Prospero intervenes. The 'Africa' that Mr Koinange served as Africa to his employers and their Western audiences is a necessity without which many illustrious international careers in the West's Mercy Industrial Complex would collapse. Chinua Achebe calls this a psychological necessity: the West *needs* to see Africa in a certain way and Mr Koinange was the perfect honorary Prospero to minister to this need.

In America as in Europe, the Mercy Industrial Complex is as important as the Military-Industrial Complex. While the Military-Industrial Complex serves the purpose of global domination, exploitation, and destruction (Freedom in US-speak), the Mercy Industrial Complex intervenes to mop up and provide the needed balm for uneasy consciences. This explains why the 'Africa' of the Jeff Koinanges of this world is so crucial not only to CNN but to the international careers of Bono, Jeffrey Sachs, Tony Blair, Angelina Jolie, Madonna, Oprah Winfrey, and the American Idol Organisation (Idol Gives Back!) in the Mercy Industrial Complex.

It is, of course, easy to demonstrate how Mr Koinange worked as honorary Prospero while the romance lasted with CNN. First is the metonymic deliberateness with which Mr Koinange served his version of 'Africa' as Africa. This is evidenced by the unmistakable nuances of his narratives. And there is the exasperating, ignorant pre-contextualising always offered by the anchors using Mr Koinange's reports: Anderson Cooper, Paula Zahn, John Roberts, Heidi Collins, and Wolf Blitzer. We have no evidence of Mr Koinange ever objecting to the inherently racist and stereotypical manner in which these anchors framed and commented on his stories.

After all, the first rule in Honorary Prospero 101 is simple: know what the white man wants to hear about Africa and feed him to his heart's content without complaining. It is not that Mr Koinange was not aware of the existence of an Africa radically different from what he sent repeatedly to CNN. No doubt he is aware of the Africa which Nigeria's erstwhile finance minister, Ngozi Okonjo-Iweala, presented so eloquently to an audience in California during her TED talk (available at http://www.ted.com/index.php/talks/view/id/127). Presenting such an Africa would have run counter to the honorary Prospero's rules of engagement. Had Mr Koinange pursued that course, he would have become a real threat to his employer, to an audience that needs to get high on news of a diseased continent, and to the Mercy Industrial Complex. Either way, Mr Koinange was bound to outlive his usefulness and crash. Such is the tragic fate of the honorary Prospero.

17

THISDAY, LAWRENCE SUMMERS, AND THE FUTURE OF AFRICA

The popular Nigerian newspaper *ThisDay* does not like to cover events and report the news as is the wont of regular newspapers all over the world. Rather, the Lagos rag loves to *make* the news it covers. And such news propositions seem to obey only one rule: ensure that the name and picture of the newspaper's founder and owner, Nduka Obaigbena, appear constantly in the neighbourhood of the globally mighty and famous. In *ThisDay* events, usually mega-advertised as the second best thing to happen to Africa after independence, it is routine to see Obaigbena beaming in the company of the likes of Naomi Campbell, Sean 'Puffy' Combs, 50 Cent, Snoop Dogg, Beyoncé, Vicente Fox, Henry Kissinger, and Paul Begala. I began to pay more than a passing attention to *ThisDay*'s dilettantism the day I stumbled on a report that arch-neoconservative pundit Bill Kristol had been part of an Obaigbena event in New York.

Now Kristol is as bad as it gets. He is one of those prurient intellects in the fundamentalist fringe of the American far right.

He is bad news for Africa; he is bad news for the rest of the world. He is interested in the rest of us only insofar as we are prepared to recognise and accept the essential goodness and desirability of American imperialism and dominion over the rest of us. We are bad news for him if we insist that no one country, no one people singularly incarnates the ultimate and final expression of the human. We are terrible news for him when we insist that he sell his exceptionalist delusions to the marines in Kandahar, or when we insist that there is no such thing as an indispensable nation. We are horrible news for Kristol when we insist that folks are welcome to define their own model of society and their values as the end of history so long as they do not foist such hallucinations on other people's narratives. Now what could Obaigbena possibly be doing in the company of such a repugnant reactionary in the cosy confines of the Waldorf Astoria?

Then comes this shocker of an announcement by the newspaper that Steve Forbes and Lawrence Summers are the two heavyweights invited 'to headline the 3rd *ThisDay* Townhall meeting on financial and stock markets holding next week in Abuja'. So far so good, you tell yourself. There is nothing wrong with two influential Americans going to discuss America's sorry economic condition while enjoying African hospitality and sunshine. Summers and Forbes probably need a break from the depressing situation back home and Obaigbena has been known to be his brother's keeper – if his brother has a name. Then this: 'Convened by *ThisDay* Board of Editors, the six-hour meeting will dig deep into the challenges of Nigeria's policy and market environment, appraise global market conditions, explore options and proffer solutions to one of the fastest growing markets in the world determined to be one of the leading global economies by Year 2020.'

In essence, Obaigbena and his editors, in their infinite wisdom, have concluded that two representatives of American

132

market fundamentalism are in the most auspicious position to perorate on 'the challenges of Nigeria's policy and market environment'. If we are lucky, the two Americans may even 'proffer solutions' to our market challenges and rocket-launch us into our desired economic nirvana in 2020, ahead of more serious and focused countries like China, India, Brazil, and the United Arab Emirates. More on this later. For now, let's dwell on Lawrence Summers and the culture that has, apparently, earned him an invitation to Nigeria.

It is difficult not to wake up every day feeling sorry for Africa. Sometimes you are sorry for what others have done and keep doing to that battered continent. At other times, you are sorry for the incredible things we Africans are capable of doing to the continent and ourselves. There is this French colonial-era police officer in Guinean writer Alioum Fantouré's 1972 novel *Le cercle des tropiques*. Taking one disgusted look at a newly independent African country already in the throes of the sanguinary dictatorship of one of francophone Africa's famous *Pères de la Nation* (Fathers of the Nation), the policeman declares that one thing that has baffled him no end in all the decades he has served in Africa is that Africans are capable of inflicting such injuries on the continent that even the most wicked white colonialist is incapable of imagining. 'You, Africans, secrete your own poison from within,' the policeman concludes.

'Colomentality' (apologies to Fela Anikulapo Kuti) is one of the most lethal poisons we secrete from within. It is a pernicious form of coloniality that Fela defines as the refusal to cure oneself of cultural and intellectual dependency on – and fascination with – everything and anything Western. It is an abdication of initiative, a voluntary surrender of agency to Western actors. Hear Fela: 'Oyinbo don release you but you never release yourself' (The white man has freed you but you are yet to free yourself). In Nigeria, colomentality is, to some extent, coterminous with Yankeephilism.

Some of the world's most uncritical Yankeephiliacs are in Nigeria. In government and elite circles, Yankeephilism is an epidemic. One comical instance: On assuming office, Segun Adeniyi, President Yar'Adua's public microphone, immediately ran to Washington for a training course, which he justified by stating that Americans were in the best position to teach him how to communicate effectively with the Nigerian people. Had his Yankeephilic exuberance not been checked by critics, he was well on his way to declaring that the Americans were the most qualified to teach him the accent and inflections of Nigerian pidgin English.

This is the culture that has ensured that any American fortunate enough to land in Nigeria becomes a demigod. When the American is white, the sky is the limit. Colomentality is what makes us assume that every American, from the uncultured college dropouts at the consular section of the American Embassy in Lagos to the highest-placed World Bank or White House official, is either an Africanist proper or an Africanist honoris causa, and therefore deserves a platform to 'proffer ideas' on the way forward for Nigeria and Africa. Folks who should be flipping burgers in New York are chauffeured around Lagos and Abuja as American expatriates, sometimes with police guards. Regular Joes and Janes who, back home in the US, wouldn't have access to the mayor of Altoona, Pennsylvania, enjoy unfettered access to our ministers and federal government officials, who suddenly become obsequious.

When colomentality sets in and surges on all cylinders, we fail to ask crucial questions about the bona fides of the Americans we are granting a platform to tell us about our lives. We fail to ask the sort of questions that would have led Obaigbena and *ThisDay* to Lawrence Summers's terrible record on Africa and the global South. Obaigbena was perhaps too smitten by Summers's profile – former vice president of the World Bank, former Clinton administration official, former president of Harvard University, former this, former that – and the prospects of photo ops to bother with trivial details in the man's trajectory. Trivial details such as what Summers thinks of the brains of American women. Fortunately, American women did not take his insults lying low. They exposed him as a radioactive male chauvinist and got him thrown out of office as president of Harvard University. Deservedly.

Yet, those angry American women ought to consider themselves lucky that Summers believes only that their brains are biologically inferior to those of their husbands, sons, and boyfriends. Africa and the global South fare much worse than biological inferiority in Summersville. While American women deserve some space in the sun as cerebrally inferior human beings, Summers doesn't extend the same generosity to Africa and the global South. In the most cynical version of economic Darwinism ever to assault our sense of decency, Summers authored – or merely signed, as he later claimed – a World Bank memo that outlined the economic benefits of dumping the toxic and industrial wastes of rich Western countries in the less-developed countries of Africa and the global South. Summers's memo leaked and caused a tsunami in global environmental circles. It is worth reproducing in full for the benefit of Obaigbena and *ThisDay*:[16]

DATE: December 12, 1991
TO: Distribution
FR: Lawrence H. Summers
Subject: GEP
'Dirty' Industries: Just between you and me, shouldn't the World Bank be encouraging MORE migration of the dirty industries to the LDCs [Less Developed Countries]? I can think of three reasons:
1) The measurements of the costs of health impairing

pollution depends on the foregone earnings from increased morbidity and mortality. From this point of view a given amount of health impairing pollution should be done in the country with the lowest cost, which will be the country with the lowest wages. I think the economic logic behind dumping a load of toxic waste in the lowest wage country is impeccable and we should face up to that.

2) The costs of pollution are likely to be non-linear as the initial increments of pollution probably have very low cost. I've always thought that under-populated countries in Africa are vastly UNDER-polluted, their air quality is probably vastly inefficiently low compared to Los Angeles or Mexico City. Only the lamentable facts that so much pollution is generated by non-tradable industries (transport, electrical generation) and that the unit transport costs of solid waste are so high prevent world welfare enhancing trade in air pollution and waste.

3) The demand for a clean environment for aesthetic and health reasons is likely to have very high income elasticity. The concern over an agent that causes a one in a million change in the odds of prostate cancer is obviously going to be much higher in a country where people survive to get prostate cancer than in a country where under 5 mortality is 200 per thousand. Also, much of the concern over industrial atmosphere discharge is about visibility impairing particulates. These discharges may have very little direct health impact. Clearly trade in goods that embody aesthetic pollution concerns could be welfare enhancing. While production is mobile the consumption of pretty air is a non-tradable.

The problem with the arguments against all of these proposals for more pollution in LDCs (intrinsic rights to certain goods, moral reasons, social concerns, lack of adequate markets, etc.) could be turned around and used more or less effectively against every Bank proposal for liberalisation.

Summers's esoteric World Bank-speak needs to be translated to English. He is simply making an economically sound argument for the violation of the environment and humanity of the peoples of Africa and the global South by the rich countries of the global North. Africans already live short, nasty, and brutish Hobbesian lives anyway. They are ragged and hungry and disease-ridden anyway. Their environment is already polluted anyway. Their life expectancy is nothing to write home about anyway. Why not save superior, more valuable lives and the environment in the West by taking the industrial wastes of the West to Africa? No crime would have been committed, no moral considerations violated, since they die down there like fowls from poverty, hunger, and disease anyway. There can be no better toilet for the rich global North than the poor global South.

The Third World's response to Summers's lunacy came from Brazil. After the memo became public in February 1992, Brazil's then secretary of the environment, José Lutzenburger, fired an angry and well-publicised letter to Summers:

> Your reasoning is perfectly logical but totally insane. Your thoughts provide a concrete example of the unbelievable alienation, reductionist thinking, social ruthlessness, and the arrogant ignorance of many conventional 'economists' concerning the nature of the world we live in. If the World Bank keeps you as Vice President, it will lose all credibility. To me it would confirm what I often said: the best thing that could happen would be for the Bank to disappear.

Summers's bona fides as an Africanist can thus be summarised in two words: psychotic Darwinism. This is the sort of character *ThisDay* is inviting to Abuja to help Nigeria figure out a way of becoming one of the best economies in the world in 2020. Apart from the sense of continental pride and dignity that should make any self-respecting African want to keep a character like Summers as far away from the continent as possible, it is ironic that Obaigbena and *ThisDay* could find no other saviours for Nigeria's market and financial system other than two apostles of the philosophy that has ruined the economy of the world's most powerful state in a little less than eight years. Summers and Forbes are epistemic participants in the process that has produced the world's biggest mendicant economy, totally dependent on loans and handouts from China, Saudi Arabia, and the United Arab Emirates to be able to continue to live above its means.

Given the current situation in the US, are these two American prophets of capital really in a position to lecture Africa about finance and economics? Shouldn't Americans rather be learning one or two lessons from the rest of us at the moment? Given their belief in market fundamentalism, what exactly are Forbes and Summers going to say in Abuja that Obaigbena could not have downloaded for free from the websites of the World Bank and the IMF? The good news about Washington's arrogant neoliberal prescriptions for Africa is that they never change. Bretton Woods and her prophets have only one all-purpose aspirin for every African ailment and the prescription is available for free on any good financial website.

If Obaigbena and *ThisDay* are that desperate for neoliberal prescriptions, I can save them some money by telling them – for free – what Summers and Forbes will tell them in Abuja. Here we go. If you guys want to join the Ivy League of global economies by the year 2020, more deregulation is the answer! Open up your markets to our products. Market! Market!! I say m-a-r-k-e-t!!! Somebody shout amen! What is this we hear that your federal government still subsidises petroleum products for the Nigerian people? When did government become Father Christmas? What is this we hear that you still have federal universities that receive government subvention? Nonsense. Open up your educational sector to market forces. Open up health, environment, natural resources – everything – to market forces. Export more of your raw materials and skilled labour at cheaper prices to the West.

And what is this we hear about boosting local production? Nonsense. Import everything from us at market-determined prices. Labour in Nigeria is unionised? You guys are kidding, right? And we hear that ChevronTexaco, Halliburton and other US multinationals pay taxes when they do business in Nigeria. Bad idea. You must make Nigeria more tax- and investment-friendly. By the way, you must open up the Niger Delta to AFRICOM so that your problem of terrorism can be solved once and for all. And while we are it, why do China, Russia, Iran, Venezuela, and Cuba have embassies in Nigeria? You cannot achieve your Vision 2020 if you associate with such vermin.

There is so much resentment, helplessness, and gnashing of teeth in Washington over the intolerable ascendancy of the BRIC economies (Brazil, Russia, India, and China). BRIC is seen as the most formidable threat to America's global dominance. While it is already too late to contain BRIC, Africa is still containable. Why anyone would imagine that two products of America's ideology of dominance would go to Abuja and teach Nigerians how to become a viable threat – like BRIC – to America's economic dominance by the year 2020 beats me. Professor Ngozi Okonjo-Iweala would have offered more genuine insights to Obaigbena and his audience. She has a stake in Nigeria's and Africa's progress that Summers and Forbes will never have. And if we must bring in non-Nigerian experts, we should have assembled some of the best brains and economists from Ghana, Botswana, and post-war Angola, three better organised and more successful countries that have relevant lessons to teach Nigeria. Perhaps I'm dreaming. It is more likely that the folks at *ThisDay* would look down on those African countries. The giant of Africa may only learn from the giant of the world!

18

A BASKETFUL OF WATER

My good friend Moses Ochonu, a professor of African history at Vanderbilt University, once penned an essay about the frustrations of offering balanced and optimistic perspectives on the Nigerian condition, even in the context of 'considerably lowered' expectations. Prior to a trip to Nigeria, Ochonu had taken the precaution of fortifying his psyche against the trauma of disappointment by lowering his expectations in line with what he deemed would be the quality of the social contract between a tragically atrophied African state and her citizens.

He tried not to expect good roads; he tried not to expect a stable power supply; he tried not to expect water from the taps; he tried not to expect safety of life and property; he tried not to expect smooth delivery of any of those routine services the state renders to the citizen; he tried not to expect courtesy from public officials; he tried not to expect people not to demand bribes. In essence, he prepared himself mentally for a trip to, well, maybe not exactly hell, but to the famed threshold between earth and hell in Yoruba mythology.

Although not quite in hell, the inhabitants of this liminal zone are sufficiently close to it to feel the heat, as we see in some of the novels of D.O. Fagunwa. To protect himself, Ochonu placed the bar of expectation so low as to bury it in the sand. Yet Nigeria managed to burrow deep into Ochonu's sand, find that buried bar of expectation, and settle down comfortably below it. In the light of this situation, my friend agonised over the dilemma of teaching Africa positively in the North American classroom when quotidian details keep pulling the rug from beneath the feet of even the most unrepentant Afro-optimist.

A few days after I read Ochonu's piece, pondering how brilliantly it mirrors my own experience, another colleague, a francophone African national, phoned from the US. As he had just returned from a trip to Zimbabwe, we talked Africa. He had not read Ochonu's piece, but what he had to say revealed an extraordinary convergence of opinions between him and Ochonu. He told me he'd perfected a 'mental survival kit' for travelling in Africa. He watches very closely the screened flight indicator in the plane. Once he notices that the plane has entered the airspace of the African continent, he takes off what he calls his 'toga of Western standards' and wears his *danshiki* of considerably diminished expectations. That way, he's never disappointed. On the contrary, he's even pleasantly surprised whenever things work. That's the only way this seasoned Afro-optimist maintains his sanity when criss-crossing the continent.

The normalisation of the substandard in Africa, its osmotic seepage into the weft of continental modes of being, can sometimes provide material for Nobel-class comedy. Accused of organising the worst-run election in human history, Olusegun Obasanjo, Nigeria's immediate past president and current national joke, lashed out at the international community for criticising an election that satisfied African standards! How can rational people expect an African election to measure up to international standards? Obasanjo fumed.

His opinion was promptly supported by Lady Lynda Chalker, the talkative British leech who always arranges to be in the company of the most reactionary elements within Nigeria's ruling cabal. The elections were indeed very successful by Nigerian and African standards, she crooned. Our humiliation was complete. Bless her soul! The old lady wasn't to blame. Our leaders delivered to her on a platter of gold the mouth with which to abuse us.

I once took a taxi from Lomé to Kpalimé in Togo. It was a standard Peugeot 505 car meant for a driver and four passengers. As is customary in so many parts of the continent, the driver squeezed two passengers in front and sardined four in the back for a total of seven people in a car meant for five. When I drew attention to this, the driver laughed heartily and gave me a paternal response: *'Ca c'est pour les blancs'* (Those standards are for white people).

Nowhere is this production of comedy out of the monumental tragedies of the African continent more palpable than in the impatience with which Africa seems to replace one negative international headline with another. Darfur supplied endless material for international headlines and gave value, sense, and meaning to the lives of Western actors operating in what I've called the Mercy Industrial Complex. While Angelina Jolie, George Clooney, and Bono were still shedding Darfur tears for international cameras, a jealous Zimbabwe drove Darfur out of the headlines. For a while, it looked like Zimbabwe was going to stay the course and spend some respectable time in the headlines, but Nigeria had other ideas. Nigeria drove Zimbabwe out of international headlines with the joke she called elections in April 2007.

As Nigeria is the giant of Africa, one would have expected other African countries to be deferential and allow her sufficient time in the sun, but Kenya had other ideas. Kenya drove Nigeria out of the headlines with even worse-run elections, effectively confirming the seminal thesis of Olusegun Obasanjo and Lynda Chalker on African elections. Before Nigerians could recover from the Kenyan affront, the shock of coming to terms with the fact that it is possible for any African country to offer a worse election scenario than Nigeria, South Africa drove Kenya out of the headlines with news of sporadic power cuts! Power outages and rationing in South Africa got less than two weeks in the international spotlight before our impatient friends in Chad drove South Africa out of the headlines. As I write, rebels have shot their way into the capital, displacing people and creating another potential refugee crisis. By now, the jet engines should be revving to move the Mercy Industrial Complex to N'Djamena until another African theatre of the absurd drives Chad out of the headlines.

If, like me, you are a scholar paid to research and teach Africa in the West, you are likely to find that Africa's generous production of negative headlines presents the most daunting professional challenge. You are a student of Eurocentrism. You are a student of the representation of Africa in the Western imagination. You are familiar with the image of Africa in the Western media. You know the tropes and metaphors of 'the Africa that never was', as the title of one famous book very aptly puts it. In scholarly circuits, you are familiar with the history and discursive trajectory of Afro-pessimism. In fact, you are part of the postcolonial, dissident, and dissentient response machine to Western traducers of our past and our present.

You prepare graduate seminars aimed at teaching your students how to approach Africa objectively; how not to pathologise Africa as eternal negation; how not to reduce the continent to a theatre of Hobbesian self-abasement among 'natives' and 'tribes'; how to sift through Western sensationalism in order to arrive at objective intellectual insights. You teach your students to be critical. You don't want them to wax positive when the facts are negative just to butter up their

African professor. You help them to establish connections between things by placing developments in Africa in the context of broader global situations and their implications.

You do this, hoping and praying that by the time they come back to class next week, Africa will not have supplied another round of headlines that could make a mess of the entire basis of your seminar. You are aware that intellectual objectivity imposes on you the recognition of the supply side of things. The Western media may sensationalise Darfur, Zimbabwe, Nigeria, and Kenya, but those countries supplied the material for sensationalisation in the first place.

Africa hardly ever disappoints. Every time my students come to class, there is a fresh set of headlines to discuss briefly before class: they always Google African news. 'What's this thing about elections in Nigeria?' I try to give answers. 'What do you make of the situation in Kenya?' I send them to The Zeleza Post to read analyses in blogs by Wandia Njoya and Paul Tiyambe Zeleza. As you answer the questions, you are boiling within. But you are not mad at them. You are in fact very happy that they take your seminar and Africa sufficiently seriously to do that extra reading in African current affairs.

Deep down, you know you are mad at Africa for the endless supply of the macabre. At times you feel so empty and drained that you begin to wonder if your self-imposed task of Afro-optimism makes you look like that funny character in the Yoruba folk tale who spends his/her life trying to fill a basket with water. That proverb may be the answer of the Yoruba people to the myth of Sisyphus. Every time you give an Afro-optimist lecture, the continent supplies new headlines to puncture your optimism, but you keep on pouring water into that basket. Stubbornly. Your love story with Africa keeps you going. Love, hope, and faith convince you that you may one day fill that basket.

19

RELIGIOUS INTOLERANCE IN AFRICA: LESSONS FROM YORUBA 'PAGANISM'

If you are Yoruba and you are older than the Facebook or Twitter generation of Nigerians, if you are struggling to cope with expressions such as LOL (laugh out loud), LMAO (laugh my ass off), and OMG (Oh my God) in emails and texts you receive daily from Nigerians in their teens and twenties, chances are you grew up in a village in Yoruba land where life is suffused in culture, tradition, and a panoply of ancestral rituals and spiritual observances, all instances of man shaping order out of primordial chaos. Chances are that, growing up, you partook – as audience or celebrant – in a very colourful tapestry of ancestral liturgies: Ogun festival, Sango festival, Imole festival, Egungun festival, and, of course, Oro festival, the fear of which is the beginning of wisdom for Yoruba women.

Chances are you enjoyed the atmospherics of these observances, partook of propitiatory offal, sang and danced to a host of inspirational choruses and processionals welcoming the ancestors and the *orishas* (deities in the Yoruba pantheon) into the realm of unworthy mortals at each spiritual enactment. Chances are you remember the sombre baritone of the officiating Ifa priest chanting '*Orisha Yoruba o, e ma ku abo o*'; chances are you remember him chanting '*Aji gini, arin gini, l'oruko Orunmila, Orunmila Baba Ifa, Ifa la o pe, Orunmila la o bo*'; chances are you remember the solemn chimes of his bell as he intones '*Kango kango, mo ma gb'ohun agogo, kange kange mo ma gb'ohun orisha o*'; chances are you remember one of the most famous of these inspirational choruses, the processional canticle of Oro:

> *Oro ile wa la wa nse o*
> *Esin kan o pe (oh eh)*
> *Esin kan o pe k'awa ma s'oro*
> *Oro ile wa la wa nse o*

It's been years now and memories flood through the grey mist of time as you remember these hymns. You do not wish to insult any of the hymns with a translation into English. No European language is deep enough to bear the full weight of these songs without doing irreparable damage to them. After all, the poverty of the English language is what made Wole Soyinka abandon his dream of translating all of D.O. Fagunwa's novels. The poor Soyinka held a rapid dialogue with his legs after translating only one of them! But you know that the Oro canticle is too crucial to the lesson that the belief system of the Yoruba has to teach contemporary Nigeria to be left untranslated. You know you must attempt to capture the soul and spirit of the hymn, while hoping that the ancestors will not fine you twenty-five cows for this miserable result in English:

> Behold Oro! The ritual of our forebears!
> Oro hampers no faith

Let no faith hamper Oro
Behold Oro! The ritual of our forebears!

You probably sang this song throughout your childhood and early adulthood; you got acquainted with new versions of it that were mainstreamed into Yoruba popular culture by traditional musicians such as Alhaji Chief Professor-Master General Kollington Ayinla, Alhaji Agba Chief Dr Sikiru Ayinde Barrister, Ambassador Oodua Abass Akande omo Rapala, and so many others; you sang versions of it that were funkified by campus social clubs while you were an undergraduate. But through all these renderings, not once did you ever pause to examine the song for its philosophical ramifications. Not once did you really listen to what it tells you about the cultural fount from which it sprang. You never analysed the hymn because you are probably not used to doing a close reading of your culture. You probably never even thought of it as a hymn. Right now, if you are an African Pentecostal Christian of the new generation, you are probably wincing in horror at the 'blasphemy' of my calling a 'pagan' song a hymn or an inspirational chorus.

If your ecumenical anger allows you to continue reading, consider this powerful line in the hymn: *Esin kan o pe k'awa ma s'oro.* I have translated what it says and what it leaves unsaid but implied: 'Oro hampers no faith. Let no faith hamper Oro.' Here we encounter the first indication of the intrinsic humanism of Yoruba spirituality: the valuation of pluralism. We encounter consciousness and validation of the spiritual essence of the Other. Indeed, we are in the presence of the accommodationist ethos of the Yoruba world view. For what this Oro canticle hints at and acknowledges is the presence of other faiths in its own spiritual space of actuation. Oro is demonstrating its awareness of the politics of otherness unleashed by the intrusion of two foreign faiths into the Yoruba world. Oro is acknowledging the presence of Christianity and Islam. These two newcomers are the *esin kan* that are being subtly referenced and advised to live and let live and not hamper older forms of spiritual expression. Oro will not bother you, for there is room enough in the sky for birds to fly without colliding. Oro is extending an olive branch to one religion that claims to be a religion of peace and another that claims to have been founded by the prince of peace himself.

From their history – or rather, the history of how their pacific essence has been twisted and bloodied across centuries by ignorant and intolerant adherents – we know that Christianity and Islam are strangers to the cosmopolitan and accommodationist graciousness of this Oro processional. For no sooner had the two religions been 'let in' – à la Stanley Meets Mutesa – than they began to invest in a sanguinary politics of otherness in Nigeria and other parts of Africa. One began to manufacture infidels who must be put to the sword via purificatory jihad, and the other, tolerating no alternative paths to spirituality, decreed itself the way, the truth, and the life. The draconian take-no-prisoners philosophy of these two religions could, of course, only eventuate in their total blindness to the accommodationist humanism of Oro.

Because Christianity and Islam insist on spiritual rebirth as the only path to God or Allah, forgetting is a fundamental element of these creeds. Forgetting is, in fact, the most significant aspect of their faiths that haughty European and Arab invaders sold to Africans as they scrambled to win 'pagan' souls all over the continent. That newly minted born-again Christian or Muslim must forget his or her former 'pagan' and 'fetish' self. When the Christian forgets to forget the old self, Enoch Adeboye and Chris Oyakhilome are on hand to remind him of the importance of forgetting: '*For old things have passed away and all things have become new*' (2 Corinthians 5:17). Only this new self, born in Christ or Muhammad and approved by Europe or Saudi Arabia, is worth remembering. Nigerian Christians go a step further. This new creature must be as white as snow in the burning tropical heat of the Lagos–Ibadan expressway, where he constitutes a nuisance to public order.

What kind of self did the born-again Yoruba Christian or Muslim have to forget in order not to come short of the glory of God or Allah? The cosmopolitan, pacifist, and accommodationist self in that Oro processional hymn is what is forgotten and sacrificed. Centuries of pluralism and communalism went into the cultural construction of that self. That self was raised by a culture that taught it to always see the humanism of the Other as an extension of its own humanism. That self was socialised by ancestral sayings and adages that always celebrated difference and privileged pluralism. That self was taught that several roads lead to the market. As that self was being socialised into adulthood, no elder in the village ever told it that there is only one way, truth, and light leading to the market of spiritual efflorescence.

This explains why that self could partake of Oro festival today, felicitate with and share the dog meat of the Ogun worshipper tomorrow, and dine with the adherents of Sango next week. Where this self was a devotee of Osun, it was unthinkable that it would try to convert or kill the worshipper of Ogun. This accommodationist ethos, in a cultural context where difference is valued and otherness celebrated, is what Christianity and Islam benefited from when they arrived, only to insist that the self rooted in that world view was pagan and must be forgotten. When this self humanised by and into traditional spiritual democracy is forgotten, the new self that is born into Muslim zealotry can only see an expendable infidel in every Christian. Likewise, the new self that is born into Christian fundamentalism can only see a hell-bound unbeliever in every Muslim. *For old things have passed away ...*

Forgetting the old self – which African traditional religions insist we must remember – is perhaps the worst damage that Christianity and Islam did to the African psyche, and we are paying the price in human lives in Nigeria today. For these two religions repressed the humane, urbane, cosmopolitan, pluralist, and accommodationist self in the old order and replaced it with a narrow-minded, ignorant, egotistical, proselytising, and modern Christian or Muslim self that can only scream, 'My way or the highway!' This partly explains the murderous political Islam that holds sway in northern Nigeria and insists on being lubricated annually with the blood of our people; this partly explains the murderous Christianity in the south-south that needs the blood of children branded as witches to feel cool. Welcome to the Islam of Boko Haram and the Christianity of Helen Ukpabio. Their motto, according to Wole Soyinka, is 'I am right, therefore you are dead!' Boko Haram kills people in the name of Islam and Helen Ukpabio murders 'witch children' in the name of Christianity because the accommodationist self that could see and value the humanity of the Other in traditional religion has been forgotten. *For old things have passed away ...*

Because Oro and other Yoruba forms of spiritual expression spring from an ethos of life and democratic spiritualism that admits of pluralism, otherness, and difference, they were crucial to the survival of Yoruba people in the New World who, unlike their fundamentalist Christian and Muslim cousins in Nigeria, understood right from the bowel of the slave ship that they could not afford to forget the self. They got to Bahia de Salvador in Brazil and the white slave master insisted they forget themselves by converting to Catholicism. The same thing happened in Cuba. But the slave master did not reckon with the accommodationist and adaptive essence of the religion of these Yoruba slaves. The slaves took whatever they could from Catholicism, blended such with Yoruba religion, and gave the world the religions of Candomblé in Brazil and Santería in Cuba. By simultaneously enacting Catholic and Yoruba rituals in Candomblé and Santería, the Yoruba of the New World are screaming, *'Esin kan o pe k'awa ma s'oro!'* In Candomblé and

Santería, the Virgin Mary lives in peace with her neighbour, Yemoja; Ogun does not grumble about the goings and comings of Saint Peter; Jesus Christ does not label Obatala a pagan deity. Candomblé and Santería are inscriptions of the old self into new things. *For old things have passed away ...*

Harmony. Harmony. Harmony. Do the Christian and Muslim fundamentalists of the old Yoruba land in Nigeria know how to listen to these things from their 'pagan' cousins in the Americas? Sadly, the Yoruba who know the meaning of Hubert Ogunde's warning, 'Yoruba Ronu', are few in Nigeria. They are mostly in Brazil, Cuba, and Barbados. As long as Nigeria is peopled mainly by selves alienated from the accommodationist and pluralistic humanism of their own cultures, as long as these lost selves refuse to listen to what their cultures have to say about the validity of the multiple roads leading to the market of spirituality, Nigeria will never know peace. I have encountered that pious Hausa Muslim who knows nothing about what his pre-jihad Habe culture had to say about pluralism and tolerance before Othman dan Fodio arrived on the scene and decided to rid those cultures of pluralistic and accommodationist values which he demonised as mixing Islam with impurities. This Hausa Muslim even got angry that I asked him about pre-jihad Habe culture, something he considers haram. *For old things have passed away ...*

I have encountered that puny Igbo noise maker on the Net, whose deranged mind is so twisted that he spends his entire life railing against every non-Muslim Nigerian who rejects his blanket hatred of Islam. He deliberately takes the murderous political Islam of a lunatic fringe in northern Nigeria for the whole religion and impugns Islam in language dripping with such venom and hate as to make Osama bin Laden's language sound like a nursery rhyme. Let us assume, for the sake of argument, that Islam is one blanket enemy that this undiscriminating fool makes it out to be in his listserv fulminations. What does his Bible tell him? *'Ye have heard that it hath been said, thou shalt love thy neighbour, and hate thine enemy. But I say unto you, love your enemies, bless them that curse you, do good to them that hate you, and pray for them which despitefully use you, and persecute you'* (Matthew 5:43–44). Our friend's convenient Christianity is blind to this inconvenient biblical injunction. His Christianity is so skewed by hate that he wastes his educated mind on such brain-dead intellectual quests as trying to determine the exact statistical percentage of Muslims a Christian society needs to accommodate for there to be peace! In all that, our 'Christian' friend doesn't realise how close he is to Nazi Aryanism or Afrikaner puritanism and how far he is from his Igbo culture which advises him to let the eagle and the kite perch. *For old things have passed away …*

I have encountered that sophisticated and Westernised Yoruba who frowns in horror at the mere mention of Oro or Ogun festival. This educated but foolish Yoruba is the first to perorate about the 'backwardness' of Yoruba 'idol worship'. Combine the lost selves of these three tragic characters in one African nation-space and you get the combustibility of Nigeria. Am I implying that Christians and Muslims in Nigeria have to jettison their faith in order to recover their lost selves and save Nigeria the spectre of one and the repeated bloodshed? No. After all, I am a practising Catholic and I have never liked the argument of traditionalists who believe that a Yoruba follower of Enoch Adeboye must literally return to the shrine of Ogun to recover his lost self. The Nigerian traditionalists who push such absolutist positions commit the same error of authoritarianism and intolerance as Christians and Muslims. They forget the fundamental spiritual democracy of the Yoruba world view which allows people to elect which deity to serve and make theirs. The Yoruba who elects God or Allah is in line with this spiritual democracy.

But this Christian must know to draw the line if Enoch

Adeboye insists that the selves humanised by Yoruba culture are nothing but idolatrous dominions, powers, and principalities that must be routed into oblivion by onward Christian soldiers; that Muslim must know to draw the line if his imam tells him to go and destroy the 'pagan shrine' of Moremi in Offa. Loss of the self is a price that only foolish people pay to buy modernity. The Chinese, South Koreans, and Japanese who today make Europeans and Americans look like Boy Scouts in the arena of techno-rational modernity did not achieve that feat at the expense of their cultures and selves. It is, in fact, Western man who has had to quickly and wisely upgrade his palate and make it compatible with sushi, bi bim bop, and General Tso's chicken in order not to be left behind by progress.

Recovery of the self implies an unconditional acceptance of the fact that everything you need for the accommodationist efflorescence of your humanity is logged in your culture and whatever version of Christianity or Islam you embrace must accept and respect those values, not condemn them. The humanism and pluralism which our forebears valued and celebrated are not mutually exclusive with Christianity and Islam. *Esin kan o pe k'awa ma s'oro* espouses an ancestral dictum of tolerance that Nigerian Muslims and Christians need to learn from. Will they ever be sufficiently humble to admit that they have anything to learn from spiritualities that the most obdurately ignorant among them still label paganism? *For old things have passed away*!

20

PHILOSOPHISING AFRICA: RESPONSIBILITIES

I have always felt that philosophising for the African public carries more responsibility than philosophy itself. 'Philosophers', according to Karl Marx's famous conclusion to *Theses on Feuerbach*, 'have hitherto only interpreted the world in various ways; the point is to change it.' This axiom presupposes a number of fundamental caveats. The act of interpretation implies the acquisition and ordering of knowledge in order to generate desired realities and narratives. Interpretation is knowing, which never operates ex nihilo – there is always a point of departure. The world we are being asked to change by Karl Marx was first known, packaged, and narrated into specific realities by folks rooted in specific cultures and histories that enabled them to produce specific orders of knowledge and create certain universes of meaning.

When you do something as mundane as stopping your car when the traffic light goes red, you may not know it but that reflex action of yours is rooted in a long history of philosophising about the interface between individual agency, civic belonging, responsibility, submission of the self to the hegemony of rules and regulations collectively agreed upon – deviation from which eventuates in established protocols of discipline and punishment. In essence, you stopped at that red light because persons as disparate as Michel Foucault, Jean-Jacques Rousseau, Voltaire, Montesquieu, and so many others *philosophised*. It is even possible to extend this filiation of thought all the way back to the Greeks, showing how a concatenation of philosophical thought you may not even care about made you apply the brakes at the red light.

What I hope to have done minimally and in passing in the preceding paragraph is to calm the anxieties of not a few participants in Africanist public discourse who invade Nigerian Internet forums with rather ill-informed comments about the futility of writing and thought in relation to the current Nigerian situation. Often, you encounter funny comments like, 'We don't need writers and thinkers. What we need right now is action!' Such commentators proceed from this fundamental illogic to dream of a Nigeria where things would 'work', as in Europe, America, and other advanced societies. As if they have ever encountered a society anywhere in history whose advancement into techno-rational modernity was not rooted in thought and writing!

These Nigerians salivate over the order, neon, and gloss of Europe and America but do not connect these things to the body of foundational thought and writing that guided these societies from the Middle Ages or to the fact that the thinkers and writers of the Meiji Restoration (1868–1912) wrote, thought, and imagined into reality the Japan they see today. Okey Ndibe, Odia Ofeimun, Wale Adebanwi, and other Nigerian public intellectuals are irrelevant because all they do is write and *whine*, but we need action right now, not whiners! We must tell these naive fellas that all the societies they salivate

155

over emerged because they were *philosophised* first by 'whiners' like Ndibe, Ofeimun, and Adebanwi.

To philosophise means to rebel in the domain of interpretation of phenomena. From the ancient times to our days, the philosopher has always been the man or woman who doubted, who queried, who restlessly said no. Descartes, Nietzsche, Sartre, and all the world's great prophets and interpreters were all fundamentally doubters and rebels, some of whom even paid with their lives. In his influential 1951 book *The Rebel*, Albert Camus uses rebellion and revolution as grids for tying together the writings and thought of an expansive array of Western thinkers and writers. What do those who philosophise rebel against? What do they doubt? What do they reject? What do they question?

If you look at history, you will be sure to find that philosopher who doubted or rejected the totality of thought and interpretations that preceded him: Friedrich Nietzsche doubted and killed the Christian god; Maurice Merleau-Ponty proposed phenomenological alternatives to the core ideas of René Descartes; there could be that philosopher who rejects aspects of or even the totality of his people's norms, cultures, rites, and other established modalities of experiencing the human; you could even have that doubter and rejecter of entrenched heritage and inheritances such as Martin Heidegger; there could even be that rebel who is not so much interested in doubting the past as in rejecting much or all of what his contemporaries and people have to say – Raymond Aron.

In essence, because they are rebels, those who have philosophised across the ages have never been afraid to say, 'My people are wrong to see or do things this or that way'. *My people are wrong*. That is a weighty statement that demands a little examination. The first point we must establish very firmly is that the philosopher – no matter how radical and countercultural – does not make the shift from 'My people are wrong' to 'My people are collective imbeciles and/or psychologically deficient juveniles'. Second, the philosopher who says, 'My people are wrong' often has specific fragments or sections of society in mind – fellow thinkers and interpreters, the politico-economic elite, the religious leadership, men, women, adults, or even the peasantry – hardly ever a totality without an exception.

When you encounter a philosopher lumping people or societies into an undiscriminating basket of collective denigration, he is more often than not talking about other societies, other people, not his. Witness Hegel on Africa and blacks. Witness Wole Soyinka's different procedure: recently, he disagreed with 'his people' in specific, unmistakable reference to an infinitesimal fragment of Yoruba peoplehood – some voices in the Yoruba Council of Elders. Never willing to read things correctly and in context, mischievous ethnicist hee-hawers ran away with his statement and proceeded to excuse the man from the collective damnation they routinely reserve for his people. Soyinka thus became the only Yoruba soul to make it to their Noah's ark and escape the flood.

Why do Soyinka and the generations of thinkers before him who have philosophised rebelliously from across every culture indulge in nuance? At the height of his career, Jean-Paul Sartre was too globally famous and influential to be touched by anybody no matter what he wrote or said. He could condemn the entirety of French history, culture, and civilisation and get away with it. When the Nobel committee awarded him the Nobel Prize for Literature in 1964, he flung it back in their faces and got away with it. He was that powerful. But he remained nuanced and discerning in his recriminations of France and the white race, whether he was condemning the brutality of France in Vietnam or Algeria, whether he was philosophising against colonisation in general, whether he was writing the most celebrated essay to introduce *Négritude* to the world, or whether he was writing introductions to the books of Frantz Fanon. Why the nuance?

Why the discernment? Why the avoidance of collective baskets of denigration of a people?

Those who philosophise do nuance because they understand the fact that there is no Archimedean point from which to perorate on the imagined collective deficiencies of a people. More importantly, they understand that their own thought, no matter how radical, revolutionary, or dissentient, still reflects the collective cultural and historical genius of the people they critique. They realise that all people have philosophised and that they are dealing with a body of thought and modes of interpretation that have been established and built upon through the ages, no matter how faulty. You may philosophise radically against everything your people believe and in the process may even stumble on epiphanic truths that may alter the course of history and change the direction of your people. Yet your production only becomes part of the history and culture of your people.

No Archimedean point of escape. Socrates understood that when he uttered this immortal wisdom: 'The only true knowledge comes from knowing that you know nothing.' Knowing this, he never sought to excuse himself from the purview of his own critique. He never felt he was superior to Athenians. He never sought a pedestal from which to arrogantly proclaim the superiority of his mind. He thought differently from his people, believed they were wrong on so many counts, and even died for it. Today his thought is part of Athenian-Greek-Western genius. As dissentient and critical of France as he was, Sartre is still French thought. That is how it works.

If Socrates philosophised that true knowledge devolves from the prior admission of one's ignorance, I daresay that the only foolish knowledge comes from believing that you are different from and superior to your own supposedly deficient people. This explains why, for me, no philosophy is superior to the collective genius of the Yoruba people housed in the

Ifa divination corpus. If you know what the Ifa corpus is all about, you will understand that all Yoruba artists, writers, and thinkers have ever done is to continuously amplify, interpret, and reinterpret the holistic gamut of experience lodged in the corpus. There is no understanding the philosophising we find in the works of thinkers, writers, and artists as disparate as D.O. Fagunwa, Hubert Ogunde, Duro Ladipo, Wole Soyinka, and Adebayo Faleti without an understanding of the epistemological universes of the Ifa corpus. There is more. Let's listen to Nelson Fashina:

> The subject of Ifa corpus raises a lot of fundamental questions bordering on available data on its history, myth and science. And if, I think, the entire gamut of Western theories and epistemology derives from the interactive interpretations ofethi tripod stand of philosophical knowledge (history, myth, science), then we of the humanities research in Africa need to know more about the potential wisdom and relative science encapsuled in Ifa divination, and how this may be appropriated to the postmodern life of Africa. Historically, Ifa was not a product of traditional religious fundamentalism. Rather, it was a composite corpus of human existence whose inextricable religious resorts are found in those prescribed ritual sacrifices which are not to be viewed or read as literal scripts, but as symbolic codes. And as symbolic codes, they are quasi-scientific formulas delineating by every atomic and molecular sense, the gravity, trigonometric and numeric range of Earth magnetic force energies and potential energies in measures and degrees of solution to human problems. Thus, there is need to review Ifa corpus in the context of primeval and contemporary contributions to human knowledge in science and technology rather than using Ifa like the raw palm-oil we used to eat roasted yam in my father's farm in the early sixties! Here lies a great task for contemporary researchers in African studies.

Fashina's statement is sufficiently self-explanatory. What we must add is that there are hardly any people in Africa, from the Gikuyu to the Igbo, without their own equivalent of the epistemological resources of the Ifa corpus. The difference often lies in cultural details and the peculiarities of historical trajectory. The disaster is that, unlike the Europeans and later the Asians, we did not separate the science from the history and the myth. Why we never did will forever remain in the realms of conjecture, but a few chapters of Walter Rodney's *How Europe Underdeveloped Africa* is a good starting point for understanding, never mind the watery postulations of the funny Eurocentrist who would attribute this to the congenital irresponsibility of the African.

Because I consider the Ifa corpus as complete a philosophy as can be, because I read it and see in it a people's genius in history, myth, and science in their attempts to make meaning out of primordial chaos, it follows that I do not invest in French existentialism or phenomenology because I believe that French philosophy has anything to say that I have not encountered in my forays into Ifa corpus; I do not read German idealist philosophers because I foolishly believe that they have anything to say that the Ifa corpus didn't spell out more brilliantly centuries before them; I do not read the philosophies of China and India – ancient and modern – because I believe that the explanations they propose on the mysteries of the universe and the riddle that is man are superior to what I find in the verses of the Ifa corpus. Rather, I read these other philosophies to determine how they explain phenomena differently from what I consider my own source-text: the Ifa corpus. I try to understand what informs the differences. In the process, I enrich my mind, expand my world, and marvel at the epistemological wonders of the Yoruba world.

In essence, I consider every philosophy that I read to be an ancillary to the Ifa corpus, the root from which I approach all discourses and epistemologies. Although I do this out of the conviction that no philosophy is superior to the Ifa corpus and that any philosophising that takes as its starting point the elevation of foreign knowledges and the ignorant dismissal of what one's own people have to say, I must say that I am not doing anything original. If you study the works of Africa's most famous philosophers – Kwasi Wiredu, Paulin Hountondji, Kwame Anthony Appiah, Kwame Gyekye, Odera Oruka, Segun Oladipo, Valentin Mudimbe, Theophile Obenga, P.O. Bodunrin, Emmanuel Eze, Godwin Sogolo, Sanya Osha – you will discover that their unrivalled mastery of what Western and Oriental philosophers have to say in such sub-branches of philosophy as ethics, logic, metaphysics, and epistemology is ritualistically secondary to their validation of what Africa and Africans have had to say in those areas. Kwasi Wiredu's *Cultural Universals and Particulars: An African Perspective* offers a quintessential demonstration of the procedure I am describing and should be read by those genuinely interested how Africans philosophise.

If professional African philosophers, who write mostly for audiences cocooned in academia, work in full consciousness of nuance, it follows therefore that if you, like Ozodiobi Osuji, elect to instruct the general public by philosophising Africa for it in easy-access online format, you must do a number of things. First, you must make sure you have read the books you recommend routinely as 'further reading' at the end of most of your essays. Even if none of the stuff you write can stand preliminary peer-review by the most elementary journal in the field, you still need to respect your audience at ChatAfrikArticles .com by getting your references right. No self-respecting public philosopher of African descent should be caught dead misspelling the names of Frantz Fanon and the irritant, Octave Mannoni, while recommending them to the public for further reading. Getting your references right is, of course, only just the beginning if you want to philosophise for your own people. You are welcome to suffer irredeemably from a messiah complex and to believe that you have been anointed to rescue your people from whatever afflictions your conjurer's handbook told you they all suffer from without exception. Just don't be caught dead writing asinine sentences like this about any people, any African people – and certainly not your own people:

> Igbos are truly a childish people; one must help them become adults but not relate to them as one's equal.

> Igbos remind me of folks mental health professionals call multiple personality disordered.

> As an Africanist, I have not seen an Igbo Africanist that I respect. This is probably due to Igbo identity crisis, their not knowing whether they are Africans or whatever they want to become.

This, I guess, seals the fate of Africanists like Michael Echeruo, Chinweizu, Emmanuel Obiechina, Ernest Emenyonu, Chimalum Nwankwo, and Obioma Nnaemeka. I meet some of these senior colleagues annually at the African Literature Association conference. The last I consider and have always related to as a sister. I never knew that these Africanists must not be respected because they suffer from an identity crisis and do not know whether they are Africans or not. And who is this 'Africanist' that one never meets in the regular circuits (professional gatherings of Africanists) of the field in North America but who singularly decides which Africanist deserves respect or not? Of course, when a Druid mixes undigested German idealism with ill-comprehended French existentialism, the end result can only be the highfalutin verbiage that is so often the fate of the 'philosophy' audience of ChatAfrikArticles.com. Here is how another thinker writes about this same people who are constantly and routinely philosophised with the vocabulary of mental health disorders in Osujiville:

> Indeed, in one of his greatest acts of overreach, Amadioha displaced the shrines/temples of Anyanwu the sun-god ... and decreed his own deification by theologising that the sun god as an all seeing universal deity required no shrine since He was already immanent and everywhere. It was he, Amadioha, who in attempts to domesticate energy and create a silver bullet for conquest, experimented with rocketry ('Egbe Elu Igwe'), created 'nsi Egbe' (gunpowder and other fissile materials) and caused the first fissile cataclysm that led to the destruction of the first human civilisation by flooding. In his experiments with energy ('ike'), he blew himself and his scientists and engineers skyward into smithereens.

Our thinker this time is Professor Obi Nwakanma, who needs no introduction to Nigerian audiences. He is philosophising the history, the myth, and the science for the Igbo world in much the same way as we encountered it earlier in the thoughts of Nelson Fashina in respect of the Yoruba world. Do the African people we encounter at the centre of Nwakanma's philosophising look anything like the people we always encounter in Osujiville?

You are probably familiar with Sango's theory of and experimentations with electricity and rocketry in the Yoruba world. Perhaps you have read Marcel Griaule's famous book *Conversations with Ogotemmeli* and you know about the Dogon people of Mali. The Dogons are famous for their monumental knowledge of astrology, especially the Sirius star system, which is the centre of their religious teachings. The Dogons have long known that Sirius A, the brightest star in our firmament, is next to a small white dwarf called Sirius B, which was identified by Western scientists only in the nineteenth century. The Dogons knew about it some one thousand years before modern/Western science 'discovered' it (and it wasn't even photographed until 1970)! Sirius B has been the basis of the most sacred Dogon beliefs since antiquity. The Dogons go as far as describing a third star in the Sirius system, called Emme Ya, which, to date, has not been identified by astronomers. Dogon mythology also includes Saturn's rings and Jupiter's four major moons. The Dogons have four calendars, for the sun, moon, Sirius, and Venus, and have long known that planets orbit the sun.

What do the perspectives of Fashina, Nwakanma, and Ogotemmeli tell us about the Yoruba, Igbo, and Dogon worlds? It tells us that our ancestors were not the pre-rational and pre-logical fools we encounter in Osujiville. It tells us that our ancestors were no strangers to science. It tells us that our ancestors played their part in the marketplace of explanations of man and phenomena. We are the ones who have tragically failed to build on their foundation by separating the science from the myth and the history. What is the role of the public philosopher who knows all these details about the African world? Insist that every African without exception is irresponsible and all we have ever contributed to history and civilisation is selling our people to slavery? Insist that Africans are congenitally inferior to the German, Indian, and Chinese philosophers you read and misapply, while deluding yourself that you are the only who reads them? What is intellectual responsibility? Must one philosophise if all one has to offer are fallacies spiced up as knowledge and erudition?

Above all, how should I process these weekly sorties in faux philosophising at ChatAfrikArticles.com and other Nigerian cyberspaces? Because I am not Igbo, I may take dangerous comfort and pleasure in the epistemic violence that the Igbo suffer routinely in the writings of a prodigal son on a rampage against his race. I may elect to object only when he extends his riotous tar brush to Nigerians and Africans as he routinely does in the name of philosophy. That would be the wrong thing to do. If I embrace one ethnic group's prodigal son because of the unbelievable things he has to say about his people, then I shouldn't complain if and when a similar character from my own ethnic group goes on a cyber-rampage against his own people and is embraced by the other ethnic group.

But that is only part of the problem. What does it make of my claim to post-Enlightenment rationality and humanism if I embrace the faux philosophy that is regularly dumped at ChatAfrikArticles.com because of the politics of MAH (Mutually Assured Hatred) going on between Yoruba and Igbo cyberwarriors? How do I subsequently enter a graduate seminar and teach that grand essentialisms and unsubstantiated generalisations go against every rule of scholarly and intellectual engagement? Do I subscribe to the 'intellectual' notion that there is any people who are all collectively 'truly childish' and who deserve to be tar-brushed in registers of 'mental disorder without exception'? That would be aiding and abetting intellectual dishonesty, for those claims are not true of any African people. Should total, uncompromising rejection of Osujist tar-brushing prevent me from taking on any Igbo thinker who slips, wittingly or unwittingly, into discourses of Igbo racial and cultural superiority while trading disagreements with people of other ethnicities? No. Should I give a rat's ass about the noise-making of preprogrammed ethnicist hee-hawers who take every disagreement with an Igbo intellectual as Igbophobia? Definitely not. Should I give a rat's ass about the Hobbesian rantings of any contemptible deviant from Yoruba protocols of earned elderhood who deludes himself that any meeting of minds between a Yoruba and an Igbo thinker is racial treachery? Certainly not. In fact, such deviance from Yoruba protocols of elderhood is the subject of a full-length treatise I am working on, now that I have found an excellent specimen in America.

Philosophising for the public, then, should be about trying

to understand why and how a people in remote Mali discovered astrology almost a thousand years before the West and why the instrumentalisation of such knowledges was arrested all over the continent. Philosophising for the public should teach that Igbo fella to be proud of the genius that Obi Nwakanma has so brilliantly compressed into the passage I quoted; philosophising should remind that Igbo fella that his people actually separated the science from the myth and the history during the civil war when necessity forced them into the creation of their own weaponry and that that truncated process of scientific creativity can still be resumed. Philosophising for the public should be about helping that 'modern' Yoruba fella understand that no philosophical text is superior to the Ifa corpus produced by the genius of his people; that the Western progress and modernity he celebrates while recoiling in Christian or Islamic horror at the first mention of the Ifa corpus were also once part of a Western 'pagan' intermesh of history, myth, and science until fellas like him applied themselves and separated the science from everything else; that the microphone that his pastor uses to give him the gospel every Sunday was part of that pagan mix until the separation; that there is still room to separate that science from the Ifa corpus for the elevation of humanity if only he and I would study it, apply ourselves to a creative extraction of that knowledge, and stop dismissing it as an inferior pagan text.

PART FOUR

INTERVENTIONS

21

VIOLENCE AGAINST WOMEN IN NIGERIA: THE INTERNET AS *AMEBO*

Among the several enemies of the Internet in Nigeria are individual and institutional actors and agents for whom that invention has become a nightmare. These are people or institutions that have good reasons to curse whoever created the global network of networks. A borderless spatial republic, the Internet quarries in what used to be your private warren, drawing out and making a public spectacle of your peccadilloes like the yells of an eight-day-old baby at its christening. The Internet is indeed one patriotic *amebo* (gossip) in the service of the Nigerian people. The Nigerian state, the sharia establishment in the north, and the Pentecostal establishment in the south are some of the institutional actors that have learnt very bitter lessons and have consequently been expending considerable resources to cope with the 'meddlesomeness' of the Internet. A short history of cyberpredicaments already experienced by each of the aforementioned institutions can offer useful insights into how the Internet offers new mediations of violence against women in Nigeria.

Like all draconian apparatuses of power, the Nigerian state took considerable time to begin to get the message that, in the age of the Internet, it could no longer be in the business of exercising power as usual – the sort of brazen arrogance of power that is routine even in the so-called democratic dispensation of a typical African postcolony. Thus, while it is taken for granted that the president's health is the people's business in civilised climes and the people are consequently notified of even routine presidential medical check-ups, the Nigerian state had other ideas about President Yar'Adua's health condition. It first behaved as if Nigerians clamouring for an honest declaration on the matter of the president's health were seeking some hallowed privilege that we were all unworthy of – that is, until Olusegun Adeniyi and other mishandlers of the president's image found out that the Internet was no respecter of the cult of silence and the culture of arrogance and deceit they were weaving around the president's health issues. Often, details of his health safaris would be all over the Internet even before he stepped out of the presidential villa. Internet pressure explains in large part Mr Adeniyi's new tack of issuing hypocritical press releases on the president's health trips.

In the hands of the Internet, Pentecostalism has also 'seen pepper', to borrow a popular Nigerian expression. Contemporary Pentecostalism in Nigeria operates a theology of instant prosperity and endless miracles that has transformed it into one of the most lucrative sectors of the Nigerian economy. Instant prosperity thrives in narratives and imagery of neon, gloss, and razzmatazz woven around a deified character always known as Founder General Overseer. If the God of Nigerian Pentecostalism is not a God of poverty, as adherents of that version of Christianity insist, He nonetheless has this annoying habit of always zeroing in on the Founder General Overseer as the only example of boundless prosperity among thousands of poverty-ridden church members. Thus, the Founder General Overseer is often the only one God elects to deck in Armani suits and Ferragamo loafers, supply with posh cars that can sometimes run two hundred kilometres on empty, and ferry across the world in a private jet. Sometimes, as is the case with Chris Oyakhilome, the bonus of a fake American accent is added unto these numerous blessings. But the Internet is what we Nigerians call *amebo* – a busybody, a loudmouth, a flâneur, a voyeur, and a whistle-blower rolled into one. And so, when the Internet pokes its unwanted nose into the business of the gospel, you could have a scandal of international proportions develop around something as ordinary as a pastor buying a private jet in an ocean of poverty.

What have these scenarios got to do with violence against women in Nigeria? Just as the Internet has not spared Nigeria's current illegitimate state and the purveyors of Pentecostal hyper-prosperity, it has also not spared the social institutions and practices that are rooted in philosophies of gender victimisation and inferiorisation which almost always eventuate in violence against women in our society. The sharia establishment in northern Nigeria should know a thing or two about this. Dateline March 2002: In this day and age, the guarantors of a wholly opportunistic and political sharia in the northern part of Nigeria, who look the other way when their politicians steal millions of dollars, only to use ordinary people, especially women, as expendable instruments of propitiation, sentenced Amina Lawal to death by stoning.

They should have thought of the Internet before doing that. And because they did not think of the Internet, it burnt their fingers, burnt their toes, and burnt their turbans very badly. Suddenly, a conservative, pre-medieval, caliphal, feudal-religious establishment that is used to having its way and riding roughshod over Nigerians got itself exposed to the worst international backlash it has ever experienced as news of the possible fate of Amina Lawal spread online like the proverbial bush fire in the harmattan. Exposed and embarrassed locally and globally, the sharia establishment buckled and started looking for a face-saving way to reverse the sentence. That is one woman's life saved when the Internet acted as *amebo*.

There is Elizabeth Udoudo, a mother of two children aged five and three years respectively. Sometime in February 2008, this woman and her children had the temerity to share the road with the convoy of the state governor in Lagos. Some details on the psychology of Nigerian convoys are in order at this juncture. I have always argued that the convoy is Nigeria's worst postcolonial tragedy. In Canada and also in the United States, the convoy – or more commonly, the motorcade – is purely ceremonial, wears a human face, and respects ordinary citizens and extant speed limits. The convoy of the Nigerian government official is obscene ostentation, intimidation, unbridled arrogance, and abject alienation from the people. It is an isle of inebriation by power, an oasis of total lawlessness. In his convoy, the Nigerian government official – often an empty barrel also known locally as a 'Big Man', 'Chief', 'Alhaji', or a combination of all three – is no longer human. The speed limit of his convoy is determined by how high the speedometer of each constituent bulletproof SUV can go.

President Obama's convoy comprises his limo, a decoy limo, one or two media buses, and a few police outriders on motorcycles. That is the length of the convoy of a self-respecting local government chairman in Nigeria. At higher levels, a respectable convoy should be at least one kilometre long. I am not going to tell you the price normally invoiced for an SUV in Nigeria. You would have a heart attack. I am not going to mention the soldiers and/or stern mobile policemen wielding AK-47s and horsewhips. I am not going to tell you that many Nigerians have been crushed by the convoys of our lawless and inhumane rulers over the years. The Nigerian convoy, of course, comes with the sort of blaring siren that people elsewhere associate with the emergency services: police cars, ambulances, and fire engines. When you see a convoy and hear the wailing siren in Nigeria, you jump into a ditch or drive your car quickly off the road to allow the man of power to pass undisturbed by the people he is supposed to be serving. When the people of Nigeria eventually wake up, the convoy will be one of the first targets of their ire. It is one symbol of oppression that they need to take out. Violently if necessary.

My generous recourse to imagery here is to highlight the atmospherics of oppression in which the convoy thrives and also to give outsiders a true portrait of Nigeria's rulers and government officials since they present a totally different persona and pretend to be cultured when they come to interact with people in the West. Don't ever believe what you see or hear when Nigerian government officials come to the West grinning from ear to ear. They are just acting, or as we say in Nigeria, they are 'forming'. That is not who they are back home. There they brutalise our people daily. If you belong with the little people, you'd better not mess with the convoy of a Nigerian government official – especially if you are a woman. Elizabeth Udoudo was driving and broke this rule that is so crucial to the architecture of power and democracy in Nigeria.

Governor Ikedi Ohakim of Imo state and his convoy would broach no such violation of the rules of engagement – by a woman, for that matter! They stopped the convoy – even time stops when the ego of a big man is at stake in Nigeria – dragged her out of the car and proceeded to beat her black and blue in broad daylight and in the presence of her young children. Needless to say, Governor Ohakim and his complement of cowardly sadists did not reckon with the might of the Internet and were soon hit by a public relations nightmare as news of their barbarity travelled in blogs and listservs. So bad was the

Internet backlash that the chief press secretary to the governor deemed it necessary to subject himself to the indignity of explaining their own side of the story to the Nigerian people – a symbolic victory, if you ask me. Of course he justified everything that happened to Mrs Udoudo, chastising her for being disrespectful to constituted authority.

I don't expect that what I have called the symbolic victory of Mrs Udoudo and the Nigerian people over Governor Ohakim and his security goons will be immediately clear to people in the West. Only Nigerians would understand what it means for what we would call 'a whole state governor' to feel compelled to explain why his security detail beat up what we would call 'an ordinary woman' on a busy street in broad daylight with her children watching. Remember, we are dealing with gigantic egos inebriated by power that is not answerable to anyone.

There is Miss Uzoma Okere. Same city. Same scenario. Lagos. Convoy. Big man. Huge ego. The difference this time is that we are dealing with a top military man. Rear Admiral Harry Arogundade was being chauffeured to the officers' mess in a convoy. He was in a hurry because he had a do-or-die appointment with a bottle of beer and a bowl of pepper soup. Miss Okere committed the usual crime of being an ordinary Nigerian competing for road space with the convoy of a big man. A military man for that matter! Please remember that these offences are much more serious when the offender is 'an ordinary woman'. As was the case with Mrs Udoudo, the big man's convoy stopped and the security goons dragged Miss Okere out of her car, stripped her naked, and beat the living daylights out of her. In broad daylight in Lagos! There was one small problem, however. The rear admiral – whom the Nigerian Internet community immediately renamed a 'rare animal' – forgot about the Internet! All it took was for some passers-by to capture the sordid scene with their cellphone cameras and upload it immediately on YouTube for our rare animal to be in big trouble. So serious was the Internet backlash this time that the president even had to pretend to take an interest in the matter and promptly transferred the rare animal from Lagos to Abuja. Another hitherto unimaginable symbolic victory actuated by the Internet serving as *amebo*.

One could go on recounting stories of how the Internet creates new vistas of female agency by seriously undermining the former safe havens of career perpetrators of violence against women in Nigerian society. The Internet has truly become a formidable ally of gender rights activists in Nigeria because it makes the business of beating and stripping women naked in public a lot riskier and infinitely costlier for the perpetrators. Are you a senator or a member of the Federal House of Representatives thinking of slapping any of those female secretaries in Abuja? Think twice. If she returns the slap, you never know who might be around to give the story considerable shelf life online. Are you the otherwise popular governor of Lagos state now victimising female strippers and allowing your goons to do unmentionable things to them in detention rather than address the underlying hostile patriarchal structures that instrumentalise those women? Beware! The Internet may be your undoing.

The cyber-age has in a way turned Nigeria into one gigantic panopticon. Those of you in academe will of course remember what Jeremy Bentham and, later, Michel Foucault have to do with the idea of the panopticon. Prisons are designed in such a way as to make the prisoner feel constantly observed without knowing who is doing the observing and where the observation is coming from. The constant sense of feeling observed is internalised by the prisoner and this induces correct behaviour. Governor Ohakim, Rear Admiral Harry Arogundade, the sharianists of northern Nigeria, and other career violators of womanhood must experience the Internet as a panopticon. These people must now affect a hypocritical smile every time they meet a woman. If they frown, there is no way of telling who may post the frown on YouTube!

Ladies and gentlemen, we must not make the mistake of deifying the Internet as the ubiquitous saviour of Nigerian womanhood. That is far from my intention here. After all, Internet or no Internet, Grace Ushang was still gang-raped and murdered only last month and this underscores the need for continuous vigilance. We must also remember the fact that the Internet hasn't spared women as perpetrators of violence against women, especially institutional and symbolic violence. Such (potential) female perpetrators of violence against women have been having a rough time in cyber-Nigeria. One of the extremely rare Nigerian politicians I admire is a member of the Federal House of Representatives called Abike Dabiri. So far, I have only positive things to say about her, but I am now nervous. For good reason. Perhaps because she used to be a journalist before she morphed into one of Nigeria's brightest politicians, perhaps in onomatopoeic consonance with her last name, Dabiri dabbled recently into the extremely dangerous territory of media control by sponsoring a curious bill that has alarmed even her most ardent supporters.

Although Mrs Dabiri has argued that her bill seeks to enhance self-regulation and professionalism in the target profession, it is becoming quite apparent that she did not reckon with the eternal verities of this saying: perception is everything. And perception acquires more dangerous potency when it travels online as Mrs Dabiri is unpleasantly finding out even as I speak. Cyber-Nigeria is gradually becoming a hostile territory for her on account of that potentially dangerous bill. Those of us who maintain our trust and confidence in her are nervous and must now handle our public expressions of faith in her extremely carefully while watching her moves ever more closely. For how could she possibly not have known that her bill has the potential to make of her a female perpetrator of symbolic violence against female journalists?

Somehow, we are supposed to trust the Nigerian state! We are supposed to believe that an irresponsible state like Abuja would use laws emanating from Dabiri's bill responsibly! I foresee opportunistic men of power turning any law that results from such a bill on its head, using it against female reporters, and exclaiming, 'Well, your sister authored and sponsored the bill!' When another female journalist is overripe for a fatwa like Isioma Daniel, the sharianists of northern Nigeria would be happy to invoke Mrs Dabiri's bill and not the sharia.

Finally, at a time when the global activist community is struggling to expand the rights of women, especially in the Arab world, a Nigerian woman has for almost two years now tried to convince the Senate that Nigerian women have too much freedom, too many rights – chief among which is a woman's right to dress as she deems fit. Senator Eme Ufot Ekaette has been misusing her position as chairperson of the Senate Committee on Women to inflict violence on her fellow women by pursuing a strange 'Indecent Dressing Bill' with missionary zeal. Why are these female lawmakers enamoured of bills that are potentially dangerous to women? Unlike Mrs Dabiri, Mrs Ekaette even took the fight to have Nigerian women dress conservatively to the UN. How relieved she must be that the crazy sharianists who murdered Grace Ushang in northern Nigeria said they raped and murdered her as punishment for indecent dressing – she was wearing trousers!

22

THE VOICE OF MUTALLAB, THE HANDS OF THE DEAD

Terrorist Umar Farouk Abdul Mutallab is the ill-bred scion of privilege that was perhaps destined to be the instrument through which the dead would visit the comeuppance of sleeplessness on a certain vicious establishment that is responsible for the greatest heap of corpses in Nigeria's history. Let's be clear from the outset: I am talking about the same people that Wole Soyinka has addressed in such stellar public lectures as 'Project Nationhood: The Chosen Against All Others' and 'The Precursors of Boko Haram'.

I am talking about a certain feudal-caliphal establishment in northern Nigeria whose only investment in the Nigerian project is a lazy and parasitic dependency on other people's oil in the Niger Delta, buoyed as it were by a psychopathological obsession with illegitimate federal power on the one hand, and the mass production of poverty in their own neck of the woods on the other.

What transpired as a near tragedy for the rest of the world

and a clear tragedy for Nigeria and Nigerians – CNN's Rick Sanchez now speaks of a 'Nigerian nightmare'– on Christmas Day 2009 in Detroit may indeed be the voice of the young and stupid Mutallab. But the hands of the dead, I argue, are also actively at work in those sinewy ways that they work only in Africa to ensure that endless mytho-cosmic traffic between the worlds of the unborn, the living, and the dead. To understand what I believe is going on here, you must be willing to suspend your subscription to the explanatory authority of all the Euro-philosophical and Americo-modern analyses that have attended this event among Nigerian, African, and other pundits and, for once, let the African world view offer an explanatory grid for these things.

The African world view I have in mind here is Yoruba, my primary tool of analysis. Any Yoruba who is sufficiently familiar with his culture knows not to joke with the concept of *ro'ku*. When the family of the deceased has good reason to believe that there has been foul play in the demise of their loved one – death from natural causes is rare in Africa – they perform certain rituals – *won ro'ku* – to ensure that the spirit of the dead finds no permanent rest. Once the *ro'ku* rituals have been performed, the spirit in question quits ghostland frequently to roam earthworld in search of vengeance. Tormented by apparitions and other bizarre happenings that could even involve being flogged by invisible hands, the guilty is pushed deeper and deeper into an abyss of irrational and insane actions that may eventually result in a confession of responsibility for the demise of a particular member of the community. The relatives of the deceased who decided to *ro* the *iku* (death) of their beloved may then rest in the comfort that the dead has secured vengeance and is now also resting.

Often – and largely due to the influence of Christianity and Islam – a family may elect not to go the ostensible route of *ro'ku* rituals. But even in such cases, there is often a quiet, subterranean actuation of the belief that *ori oku a ja* (literally, 'the head of the departed') will fight and avenge itself. 'Head' is to be understood here in the African sense – something like Chinua Achebe's *chi*. Here, we are in the domain of indirect *ro'ku*, where no ritualistic actions of facilitation or mediation are required on the part of the living. The wicked people who are directly responsible for a death and the structures or people who bear indirect responsibility for the said death through actions of complicity or criminal inaction are made vulnerable to the vengeful whims of the restless and fighting 'head' of the dead.

The Yoruba say of such persons and the people or powers behind them *won o ni sinmi* – they will not (find) rest. Whether through the enactment of appropriate rituals or through simple belief in its potency, the philosophy of *ro'ku* presupposes an endless roaming of the spirit of the dead in order to occasion irrational actions among the living and the guilty. Thus, at any given point, earthworld is criss-crossed by unappeased angry souls that have not been able to find eternal rest and must deprive the guilty among the living of sleep and rest until the society of the living embraces the path of restitution and punishment.

Unappeased angry souls such as that of Gideon Akaluka, the young Igbo trader whose restless spirit has roamed and haunted the city of Kano since December 1994, *ro*-ing a death whose gruesomeness is surpassed only by the criminal shortness of Nigeria's national memory. We have simply forgotten him and moved on. Yet Mr Akaluka's family must still deal with the gory spectre of their son's head dangling from a spike in broad daylight as a mob of crazy Islamic militants danced with it through the streets of Kano, chanting *Allahu Akbar* (another Christian infidel down, some fifty million more to go in Nigeria). The mob that beheaded Akaluka in Kano had enablers and complicitous political profiteers in the northern elite and leadership. Now Akaluka is *ro*-ing his own death. The scions of the politically complicit are misbehaving. And the chicken is home to roost.

Unappeased angry souls such as that of Christianah Oluwasesin, the young Yoruba schoolteacher whose restless spirit has roamed and haunted the town of Gandu in Gombe state since March 2007, ro-ing a death whose gruesomeness is surpassed only by the criminality of Nigeria's national memory. We have simply forgotten her and moved on. Yet Ms Oluwasesin's family still deals with the gory spectre of their daughter's lifeless body, after she was clubbed to death in broad daylight by crazed Islamist pupils who accused her of desecrating the holy Koran even as they chanted *Allahu Akbar* (another Christian infidel down, some 49 999 999 more to go in Nigeria). The lynch mob in Gandu had enablers and complicitous political profiteers in the northern elite and leadership. Now Oluwasesin is ro-ing her own death. The scions of the politically complicit are misbehaving. And the chicken is home to roost.

Unappeased angry souls such as that of Grace Ushang, the twenty-five-year-old youth corper whose restless spirit has roamed and haunted the city of Maiduguri since September 2009, ro-ing a death whose gruesomeness is surpassed only by the criminality of Nigeria's national memory. We have forgotten her in less than five months and moved on. Yet Ms Ushang's family still deals with the gory spectre of their daughter's lifeless body, after she was raped and murdered by irate Islamic militants offended by the sight of her in khaki trousers – given to her by the federal government of Nigeria, a state she was serving at the time. She wore trousers in Nigeria's sharianistan and paid with her life in 2009 (another Christian infidel down, some 49 999 998 more to go in Nigeria). The mob that raped and murdered Grace Ushang has enablers and complicitous political profiteers in the northern elite and leadership. Now Ushang is ro-ing her own death. The scions of the politically complicit are misbehaving. And the chicken is home to roost.

Within recent memory, Gideon Akaluka, Christianah Oluwasesin, and Grace Ushang are tragic signposts on a bloody trajectory that has taken us from Maitatsine to Boko Haram, accounting for close to three decades of an annual blood fest in the name of religion in a country that will only be fifty years old in 2010. There are hundreds of thousands more where the troika of Akaluka, Oluwasesin, and Ushang came from. Hundreds of thousands of unappeased angry souls hovering over Nigeria in search of restitution and the ascription of responsibility and punishment to the guilty. Yet, in more than thirty years of regular Islamist blood fest in northern Nigeria, the federal government has never arrested and tried a single Islamic fundamentalist. As far as the cretinous status quo in Nigeria is concerned, no one was responsible for the deaths of Akaluka, Oluwasesin, and Ushang. There have been no investigations. Nothing beyond the platitudinous expressions of dismay and the promise to leave no stone unturned until the perpetrators are found.

Unknown to the political opportunists in the northern elite who manufacture the onward Muslim armies of hunger, who indoctrinate and deploy them periodically to gory and devastating ends just to maintain the status quo, and who proceed to ignore the imperative of justice for the dead, so long as the victims answer to Christian names from the south or so long as they are faceless and nameless expendable Muslim commoners from the north, every death has been a step forward on the road to Umar Farouk Abdul Mutallab. Their nonchalance and neglect of the epidemic of religious violence in northern Nigeria have now been taken to new levels. Now the dead are *ro*-ing years of injustice and criminal complicity by the northern establishment. The restless hands of the dead are at work. The spoilt children of our friends, who live in four-million-pound apartments in London, are joining Al-Qaeda and ensuring that their corrupt fathers in the Nigerian status quo will neither know peace nor find rest.

It must be said that the complicity and guilt of the northern establishment finds comfort in the attitude of the Nigerian media and intelligentsia. The imperative of naming names and ascribing responsibility for these things to specific people and fragments of Nigerian society – where evidence abounds – has always given way to clever demission and political correctness. We are always enjoined not to hold a particular religion or a particular segment of Nigeria responsible for anything. Such analyses often veer into inane philosophical abstractions on collective responsibility, systemic and institutional failure, and other academic platitudes. Reuben Abati, for instance, has written an article on the current disgrace in which he somehow manages to comfort everyone – including the Mutallab family – and blame no one in particular.

In his own refreshingly different and heartening submissions in the article 'Nigeria's Terrorism Notoriety', Okey Ndibe brilliantly analyses these issues and ascribes responsibility, but he falls just short of specifically naming the northern establishment, preferring such euphemisms as 'government', 'the Nigerian state', and 'official nonchalance towards the phenomenon of domestic religious violence'. There is a specific establishment behind 'government', 'the Nigerian state', and 'official nonchalance', and we must now name and go after them in our critical reflections. Okey and those of us on the same side in the struggle for meaning within the Nigerian conundrum must now realise that the northern establishment has learnt to count on us for such neo-Enlightenment grand gestures of conceptual liberalism. They have learnt to blackmail us as Islamophobic bigots whenever we move too close to naming them.

We must now call their bluff in our writings and name them. If we can name Helen Ukpabio and hold her responsible for murdering 'witch' children in the name of fundamentalist

Christianity, if we can name and hold the likes of Enoch Adeboye and Chris Oyakhilome responsible for a brand of fundamentalist Pentecostalism that is too cosy with the corrupt political establishment in Nigeria, we must hold a mirror to the face of the northern oligarchy. We must in fact make a conceptual shift and stop calling the annual carnage that these people condone and refuse to punish in northern Nigeria 'religious violence'. They have learnt to live with that designation. It is terrorism, pure and simple. We must call it terrorism. We owe the Nigerian people that conceptual shift. For while we are at it, trying to avoid being called bigots, all we get from those who profit politically from Nigeria's annual ritual of domestic religious terrorism is insufferable arrogance, such as we witnessed recently from one of them, Rilwanu Lukman, the irresponsible minister of petroleum resources who abandoned Nigeria to an ongoing fuel crisis to catch up on winter holidays in Vienna in clear defiance of a vice-presidential order to stay at home and work on addressing the problem.

We must insist on the fact that it is neither stereotyping nor bigotry to acknowledge and critically engage empirical and provable facts. If it is empirically provable that northern Nigerian has been the locus of virtually every incident of domestic religious terrorism since independence, if the nonchalance of northern leadership to this gory trajectory of blood is evident and provable (they have never tried anyone for any of the murders), we should go ahead and name them and damn the consequences. Let us harbour no compunction whatsoever in acknowledging the fact that the dead are *ro*-ing their own death and manufacturing Mutallabs. Let us celebrate the fact that those who have denied them justice and their humanity – justice, according to Soyinka, is the first condition of humanity – will not know sleep and peace. Where Nigerians have been incapable of doing so, the Americans will now guarantee their insomnia and heartening discomfort.

23

THE AMERICAN SOUTH
AS WARNING TO THE
NIGERIAN NORTH

In this essay I have elected to play on the title of Aleksandr
Solzhenitsyn's little-known political treatise *Warning to the
West* for good reason. Solzhenitsyn, the Soviet novelist and
winner of the 1970 Nobel Prize for Literature made famous
by his Gulag experience under Joseph Stalin, frequently had
reasons to warn the Western world in much the same way as
it has now become imperative to constantly warn the Nigerian
north. As religious fanatics in the north commenced their by
now familiar annual yam festival of wanton bloodletting in the
name of Islam, the Nigerian president announced that he had
held meetings with his service chiefs who were also in contact
with the governors of the affected Boko Haram states, notably
Bauchi, Borno, and Kano. No one suspected that he was hinting
at an orgy of indiscriminate wasting operations and purposed
extrajudicial executions as an alibi for a possible holocaust to
be visited on the Niger Delta in the foreseeable future. Security

meetings and hare-brained harassment of the government and people of Lagos state over, the president fiddled away to Brazil on one of the most tragically ill-timed state visits in history.

He should have gone on a private visit to the United States instead. He should have travelled with a large retinue of northern stakeholders. He should have travelled with just about anybody from the north with the ability to study history, read between the lines, and make the connection between things. For if there is anything the northern elite in Nigeria need more desperately at the moment than the oil of the Niger Delta, it is knowledge of the history of the American South. I am talking about the Deep South: Alabama, Georgia, Mississippi, Louisiana, and South Carolina. The leadership of northern Nigeria needs this knowledge for their own good and for the sake of Nigeria.

One could, of course, advise Mr President to stay behind in Nigeria and read the novels of William Faulkner. After all, being one of the most famous writers of the twentieth century and having won the Nobel Prize for Literature in 1949, Faulkner single-handedly placed the Deep South on the pedestal of global imagination by setting virtually all his blockbuster novels there. But not even the maximalist luxuriance of Faulkner's prose can replace the direct feel and touch of history, hence the necessity of a visit. You see, the Deep South is not also called the Cotton States for nothing. Cotton! The first hint of the dark historical underbelly of the Deep South. For who says cotton says plantation. And who says plantation says slavery. And who says slavery says it is at the base of an entire culture and political economy that developed on it – and around it.

I am not interested in the political economy of slavery. Eric Williams has adequately taken care of that in his classic book *Capitalism and Slavery*. That leaves culture. What kind of cultural imagery does the Deep South immediately evoke? There is art as in jazz and the southern cuisine of Louisiana with its Cajun/Acadian inflections. There is the musicality of the southern drawl when white southerners speak their dialect. And the beauty of raw, fast-paced Ebonics when southern blacks speak their own dialect. That's the good news. But the good news is not relevant to us here. There is also a culture of poverty and a pervading sense of backwardness and underdevelopment in relation to other parts of America, especially the northern states. Here is what I had to say about poverty and backwardness after touring the Deep South by road in the summer of 2005:

> Back in Pennsylvania, I phoned a cousin who was a student in Alabama. I told him that I needed a road trip in rural Alabama and Mississippi in the summer of 2005 to continue my education. He laughed and told me that what I mistook for black poverty in the state of New York was in fact black luxury! 'I will show you black poverty when you come to the South,' he said. He was right. We spent a whole month travelling in America's black poverty belt in the South. In certain places, it felt like the plantation was still alive and healthy. Only Massa was gone. Here were Americans poorer than anyone I have ever met in Africa. American towns and neighbourhoods more indigent than anyplace I'd seen in Africa. I travelled in those spaces where the anger that white America doesn't understand smoulders.

What I painted there was the culture of southern black poverty. Add that to the comparative material backwardness of southern whites in relation to their cousins in the American North and a picture of the Deep South emerges: it is less prosperous than the northern part of the country. For much of the contemporary history of the United States, the Deep South has been a less-developed region playing catch-up with the rest of the country. How did this happen? The American North was far less dependent on slave labour and even came to acquire a false reputation in history textbooks as the real land of the free, never mind that they also had low-scale slavery. Once the black slave escaped the tyranny of slave life in the Deep South, the inclination was to run to the land of freedom up North. The flight up North is brilliantly captured by Edward P. Jones in his 2003 Pulitzer Prize-winning novel *The Known World*. The lack of exclusive dependence on illegal slave labour and plantations by the North created a pluralistic conceptualisation of the material base of society in that part of the United States. This in turn led to a diversification of the sources of wealth creation and a boundless spirit constantly seeking more diverse ways of societal progress and advancement that would later eventuate in manufacturing and industrialisation. *Theirs was a philosophy of building society yourself.*

The white elite (the Tuckahoes) of the Deep South, on the other hand, fought a war to prevent the pluralisation and diversification of the sources of wealth creation and the material base of society. Theirs was an insipid society that could not and did not want to think beyond slaves and slavery. They also couldn't think beyond cotton. One of the least talked-about consequences of slavery in the Deep South is the emergence of a thoroughly lazy, indolent, and unimaginative southern white plantocratic elite that had grown so used to slaves doing everything for them they couldn't even wipe their own behinds after shitting. *Theirs was a philosophy of using unwilling slaves to build society.* This laziness of the Tuckahoes, induced by over-reliance on slaves and cotton, is the beginning of the wealth and development gap between the Deep South and the more industrious and diversified North. This was bound to happen. The march of history caught the white elite of the Deep South with their pants down. Slavery ended and Massa was suddenly naked. Emancipation of blacks meant that those who had never learnt to do anything on their own suddenly had to begin to imagine other ways of progress and societal advancement. They have been playing catch-up ever since.

If they are reading this, the elite in northern Nigeria should be in familiar territory by now. Replace slaves with oil and southern white elite with Hausa-Fulani elite and our plot shifts seamlessly from the American Deep South to northern Nigeria. Without oil, the elite of northern Nigeria cannot wipe their own behinds. In essence, the kind of white elite that slavery created in the Deep South is precisely what oil has created in northern Nigeria: indolent, lazy, unimaginative, and irredeemably greedy. The white elite of the Deep South even had some redeeming values: they took care of their own. Not so our friends in northern Nigeria. In more than thirty years of deranged looting of national wealth (with regular equal-opportunity windows of massive looting by southern quislings such as Olusegun Obasanjo, Andy Uba, and James Ibori), these crazy elites have turned their own people in the north into one of Africa's most poverty-beaten people. Northern Nigeria is that country's synonym for backwardness, underdevelopment, and poverty. I should know: I lived in Sokoto and Kaduna, the hearts of the caliphate.

If the white elite in the American Deep South went to war to be able to cling to slavery as the only source of wealth generation, their copycats in northern Nigeria have clung to that plot since oil was struck in the Niger Delta. They have been at war to remain unimaginatively addicted to oil and have even ordered air raids in the Niger Delta to maintain their iron grip on things. Worse, they even destroyed the pre-existing diversified base of wealth generation (from cloth dyeing to agriculture: the groundnut pyramids!) in that part of Nigeria just to concentrate on oil loot. This addiction to an unimaginative monocultural philosophy of wealth generation accounts for their maniacal determination to maintain the Stone Age federalism Nigeria operates, which over-concentrates the power to loot and mismanage oil wealth at the centre. In the process, they have created a thoroughly underdeveloped and backward northern Nigeria that is perpetually playing catch-up with the rest of the country, never mind the numerous official measures (quotas) they have foolishly adopted over the years to retard the progress of the south and close the gap.

The culture of poverty and ignorance they groom among their own people in order to sustain this scenario accounts for tragedies like Boko Haram: the northern elite must be held squarely responsible. Like the more talented white oppressors who wrote their script in the American Deep South, history is bound to catch up with the oligarchy in northern Nigeria. The history of the Deep South teaches us that the addiction gets worse as things hustle towards an inevitable end. As slavery was winding down, the vocabulary of Massa was tied even more to slaves. Take a look at the diction of Nigeria's northern elite even as the world marches inexorably towards the end of the era of oil. Although I have long lost the capacity to be shocked or scandalised by Abuja, I can't help wincing at the thought that all you hear from them now is talk of oil blocks, petroleum industry bill, petroleum training institute, petroleum university, petroleum this and petroleum that, all signals from an elite that is totally tone-deaf to the message from the rest of the civilised world that the end of oil is nigh. As I write, the leadership of northern Nigeria is still desperately prospecting for oil in the north.

Nigeria's northern elite are clinging to a vocabulary of oil at a time when the national budgets of the oil states in the Arabian Gulf are evolving towards oil independence; at a time when Moloch Yaddie is in Brazil, a country that has left oil behind and now runs on ethanol; at a time when President Obama's main agenda in office is to secure America's independence from oil; at a time when China and India have also joined the race to a future without oil. Definitely, these elites are entombed in the prison-house of oil. Things wouldn't be this frustrating if the northern elite had shown themselves capable of at least stealing intelligently. Intelligent stealing happens when, after looting over US$200 billion dollars in thirty years, we see a Dubai-like northern Nigeria with massive high-tech agricultural infrastructure that could make it the food basket of Africa. Northern Nigeria could conveniently feed the African continent. With its tomatoes, onions, potatoes, maize, guinea corn, beans, and so many other foodstuffs, this part of Nigeria has the capacity to make Canadian agriculture look like Boy Scouts agriculture had the loot of the northern elite been massively invested in it in the last three decades. And they had cotton too before they got drunk on oil. Yes, cotton! Like their teachers in the American Deep South!

Here then is the warning: Unless a brand-new generation of sufficiently dissatisfied northerners forty years old and below rise up to take radical stock of things; unless they categorically reject a dependency mentality that ties the fate of the north to the Niger Delta's oil at the expense of developing the vast agricultural and mineral potentials of Arewa land; unless they understand that our envisioned Nigeria of the future will not tolerate the retrogressive born-to-rule mentality of their elders; unless they understand that the northern leadership, as currently constituted, is too moribund to think beyond oil and too wicked to think beyond narrow class interests; unless they study how scrupulously the old and current guard of the northern elite have applied the strategies of the white slavers in the Deep South of the United States to make a total mess of the north and Nigeria; and, most importantly, unless they understand why the Deep South has had to play catch-up with the rest of America for so long, the north will continue to lag behind and play catch-up for another foreseeable century even with its stranglehold on the centre, quotas, federal character, and other foolish strategies designed to slow down the pace of development in the rest of Nigeria. Let's hope that the odious rulers of Nigeria will let her have another century.

24

BRITAIN, HISS-HISS-HISTORY, AND THE NI-NI-NIGER DELTA

'The trouble with the English,' stutters Whiskey Sisodia, a character in Salman Rushdie's famous novel *The Satanic Verses*, 'is that their hiss-hiss-history happened overseas, so they do-do-don't know what it means.' Sisodia's is, in my view, the most famous stutter in literature, offering, as it were, a priceless window into the mindset behind Prime Minister Gordon Brown's generous offer of British military assistance to Nigeria's murderous federal government to quell 'terrorism' in the Niger Delta. Naturally, Mr Brown did not stop at lecturing Nigeria's illegitimate president on the need for robust actions in the Niger Delta during the latter's ill-advised recent state visit to Britain; he even felt sufficiently enamoured to make a public show of his impatience with the situation in Nigeria. The 'terrorists' in the Niger Delta are beginning to have a serious impact on the wallets of the English whenever they approach the gas station and Mr Brown would have none of it. If President Yar'Adua has forgotten the Dan Fodian art of pacification, the

English still have one or two tricks left to teach him in that department. After all, they are history's most prolific pacifiers. Mr Brown only needs to dust off one or two volumes of the colonial library. And that is precisely what he did.

Mr Brown's offer of British munificence and President Yar'Adua's obsequious disposition in London have generated the usual Internet lather among angry and embarrassed Nigerian pundits. Such condemnations of President Yar'Adua are a tad harsh and uncharitable. If he went to London to grin from ear to ear as he was lectured on how to put his house in order, it is only because the visit to Number 10 Downing Street is the second most important day in his life, going by the logic of his own brilliant declaration that his visit to the White House last year was a day he would never forget in his life! The extraordinary privilege of being able to say 'Yes, sir' to the American president in Washington is followed closely by the celestial privilege of being able to say 'Yes, sir' to the British prime minister in London. Allah be praised! Those who expected from President Yar'Adua behaviour better than that of a three-year-old child in a candy store still have a lot to learn about the sheepishness of African leadership in the presence of their Western overlords. Let's cut President Yar'Adua some slack. He did not disappoint. He behaved admirably to type.

Now to the more serious business of his British host. I have read several engaging analyses of Gordon Brown's sudden interest and desire for peace in the Niger Delta. The thrust of most of these analyses is nicely summed up in Kennedy Emetulu's robust intervention, 'Anglo-Nigerian Relations: An Oily Romance'. We do, however, need to move things beyond the political economy of oil and bring the historical provenance of Gordon Brown's mindset to bear on our discussion in order to fully understand not only his 'ways of seeing' (apologies to John Berger) but also, and perhaps most importantly, the limited range of the vocabulary available to him to frame his idea of the Niger Delta. Put differently, whenever the Niger Delta intrudes into Gordon Brown's consciousness – as it obviously does frequently these days – how does his peculiar history, which mostly happened overseas, enable him to deal with the situation? What imagery, symbologies, and vocabulary does this history place at his disposal to frame reality? Could he have seen anything other than a military solution (final solution?) to the Niger Delta question?

Whereas history avails President Yar'Adua of only two words – *militants* and *infidels* – to describe the freedom fighters of the Niger Delta, it is even less generous with Gordon Brown. There seems to be a miserly logic to history's distribution of vocabulary in the province of oppression. The higher up you are on the ladder of oppression and historical transgressions, the more impecunious your vocabulary becomes in terms of your capacity to describe, name, and engage your victims. For instance, across the Atlantic, the theo-conservative lunatics in power can only see *terrorists*. The same historical logic makes it impossible for Gordon Brown to see either people or Nigerians in the Niger Delta. His own history avails him of only one descriptor, buried deep down in the psyche: *natives*.

But that is only part of the problem with this Englishman whose history happened everywhere except England. When his history happened in India at the expense of the Indian, he saw only natives undeserving of liberty and self-determination; when his history happened in Jamaica, cannibalistic natives haunted his dreams; when his history happened in Kenya and Zimbabwe, it was the same story of ungrateful natives indulging in violence to secure their freedom. Even female natives in Aba, Nigeria, overstepped their bounds! It is in contemplation of the natives' will to fight for freedom that history becomes a bit generous and the oppressor's vocabulary is upgraded to five words. Five words that he regurgitates repetitively to describe the actions of *his* natives: *revolt, rebellion, riot, mutiny, uprising.*

Consequently, from Morant Bay to Meerut, from Mount Kenya to the Chimurenga fields of Matabeleland, our friends the English saw only low-level, despicable actions like riots, revolts, rebellions, mutinies, and uprisings. Strange descriptions dignifying such events with names like decolonisation, liberation struggle, freedom struggle, and wars of independence would enter the picture only when the native decided to seize the narrative through the pens of African nationalists and folks like Chinua Achebe, Ngugi wa Thiong'o, and Frantz Fanon.

Well, the situation had to be addressed and the natives put in their place. History became miserly again, granting the oppressor only one word to describe his praxis: pacification. We all know how successful the pacification was in the second half of the twentieth century. After five centuries of bloodshed across the globe, history returned to its small island in England, to cower as an inconsequential entity in the shadow of the Frankenstein it created: America. This is the historical baggage that determined the atmospherics of the Brown/Yar'Adua encounter in London. Each man came to the table with a historically determined mode of perception of current reality. History is stubborn. The collapse of Empire does nothing to the atavism of its diction. Its vocabulary persists in the subconscious and the wounded psyche of Empire's scions and is surreptitiously deployed in erroneous renderings of the present. Hence, there is only one constricted formula available to Gordon Brown: in his mind, the Niger Delta is a space filled with mutinous, riotous, or rebellious natives in dire need of pacification. His history leaves him no other option of perception. That essentially is the formula he sold to a gullible Yar'Adua. Lest I forget, the resource-laden environment of the native is always more important than the native in the calculus of the oppressor.

There is, of course, the usual throng of happy African intellectuals who roam Internet listservs claiming that history has nothing to do with these things. If Mr Brown sticks his foot in his mouth, we must not look into his history. We should just explain it away as a passing bout of athlete's foot. We must look beyond the distractions of such comical intellectuals and insist that there is a name for Mr Brown's foray into the Niger Delta situation: imperialist nostalgia. One of the world's leading anthropologists, Renato Rosaldo, has a classic scholarly essay on the symptoms of this disease and I do not need to rehash his submissions here. Suffice it to say, however, that whenever the disease afflicts the English, it manifests in the shape of an uncritical reproduction of the scripts of Cecil Rhodes, one of the British Empire's greatest sons. It was Rhodes, after all, who declared that he could only conceptualise the relationship between the British and their colonised natives as the partnership between a horse and its rider. While Mr Yar'Adua and his sycophantic entourage may deceive themselves that they discussed 'friendship', 'partnership', 'cooperation', and 'bilateral agreements' with the English, my kindergarten cousin in Nigeria knows that Gordon Brown was operating from Cecil Rhodes's rule book. There can only be a partnership in which the English would be the riders and the Niger Delta the horse. That's the only way the English are able to cling to the illusion of Empire in an era when the likes of Germany and France have rendered them irrelevant even in little Europe!

Gordon Brown's strategy is going to be even more crucial to his country as we enter, thankfully, a global phase that seems to mark the beginning of the unravelling of the American Empire. It is one thing to live in the shadow of the Americans after the sun set on the Union Jack only to shine on the star-spangled banner. How does one live under the red banner of China? The British answer to the spectre of China is to ensure that their irrelevant present, like their past, happens overseas. To this end, Tony Blair and now Gordon Brown have ensured that the British present is happening tangentially to the American present in Iraq, Afghanistan, Zimbabwe, and the Niger Delta.

Empire never learns.

Let's not kid ourselves about the sorry nature of Nigeria's leadership. Mr Brown's offer will either be accepted brazenly and publicly or through the back door in some attenuated form. If President Yar'Adua opts for a brazen public acceptance, he will be counting on Nigerians' legendary capacity to make some noise before shrugging and proclaiming *God dey*. If Gordon Brown successfully pacifies the Niger Delta, I wager that Dokubo Asari, Henry Okah, Ateke Tom, Jomo Gbomo, and all the freedom fighters involved in the struggle will meet with a slightly better fate than Okonkwo, whose story ends up in 'a reasonable paragraph' in the District Commissioner's book at the end of *Things Fall Apart*. Okonkwo and Umuofia had no crude oil and could not be expected to be anything more than trivial anthropological exotica in the Englishman's book. The people of the Niger Delta are luckier. They have oil and should, hopefully, be promoted to two reasonable paragraphs in Gordon Brown's memoir.

25

PROJECT NIGERIA: THE STRUGGLE FOR MEANING

In some of my recent interventions on Project Nigeria, I framed the question of patriotism as a struggle for meaning between, on the one hand, those ponces of power in the service of the ideological apparatuses of the state with its fanciful myths and narratives and, on the other, the citizens who understand only too well that patriotism should not, under any circumstances, be allowed to become coterminous with the will, ego, desires, and agendas of the ruling elite, especially where the state is held hostage by buccaneers as is tragically the case with Nigeria. A people that lets this happen pays a terrible price. Most Americans are now considerably wiser after surrendering pertinent initiative in the struggle for meaning by allowing lunatics like Rush Limbaugh, Glenn Beck, Ann Coulter, Sean Hannity, Bill O'Reilly, Michelle Malkin, Karl Rove, Donald Rumsfeld, Paul Wolfowitz, Douglas Feith, and a gaggle of evangelical Christian fundamentalists to define patriotism for them and reduce it to an unquestioning faith in the cerebral debilities of George Walker

Bush and Dick Cheney. An eight-year reign of neoconservative ideological terrorism was the price of that American concession in the field of meaning. Sadly, the rest of the world also suffered the consequences along with Americans.

My submissions attracted very interesting and engaging responses from a broad spectrum of readers from within and without academia. I am interested here in some of the extremely interesting insights that came up in subsequent exchanges with non-academic respondents. In such exchanges I learnt invaluable lessons about the need to de-ghettoise academic labour, bring it down from its perch on Mount Olympus, and make it speak with and to the world outside, rather than in the endless monotonous drone it generates by claiming meaning only for itself within the confines of the ivory tower. Three respondents took the time to grill me on my constant reference to Project Nigeria as a struggle for meaning, asking me to demonstrate, in concrete terms, how this undefined and slippery struggle for meaning translates to the albatross I'm making it out to be. One of the respondents, an intellectual in his own right who is not currently in academe, wondered if I was coming from Paulin Hountondji's submissions in his seminal book *The Struggle for Meaning*.

Although I have read the eminent African philosopher's book, I do not come to the struggle for meaning from the perspective of Hountondji's work. I am coming from the earlier work of Joshua Lund, a theorist of Latin America, whose work on the struggle for meaning has contributed significantly to our understanding of the fact that the first thing the native peoples of the Americas lost to Christopher Columbus and other marauding Europeans from Spain, Portugal, France, and England was not land and territory, as is conventionally understood, but meaning and the power to make land, culture, and the environment *mean*. This original loss was to frame the modalities of imagining that legitimised Anglo-European ways of being, especially in the United States and Canada, and establish a continuum of instrumentalisation of the original owners of the land. It is a pointer to who won and who lost the struggle for meaning that the Anglo-American conquerors of Native Americans subsequently developed a flair for naming mechanical things that they ride after the Indian tribes they exterminated. Today, many Americans ride Cherokee Jeeps, Pontiacs, Dodge Dakotas; their military flies Apache, Comanche, and Chinook helicopters. Nobody remembers that these are all names of vanquished Indian tribes ... except the Indians, who mostly cannot afford the motorised devices that are so named to add insult to injury by reminding them that they lost the struggle for meaning.

If you remove the fact that the Nigerian people today are dealing not with European conquerors but with much deadlier internal colonisers, our condition replicates the essential features of the Native American situation in terms of the loss of the struggle for meaning to a fissiparous ruling elite that got the first and only shot at making Nigeria mean in the build-up to independence and proceeded to mal-define Nigeria's foundational national myth as a reflection of the primal needs of the belly – the belly of their class. There is no nation without a foundational national myth. When that myth commands the attention and respect of the citizenry, it garners legitimacy and hegemony as leadership and followership come to subscribe to it as the fundamental identity of a perpetually unfinished nation. It becomes the most solemn definition of what that nation is about, who the people are and where they are headed with project nationhood. The national myth is the ultimate locus of difference. It differentiates one nation from every other nation.

For Americans, it is the idea of their nation as the ultimate land of dreams – the American dream. No American jokes with this solemn definition of his/her country. They have spent more than two hundred years working continuously to make that expression mean for every American. And they pack everything that defines the essence of the human into that national myth – freedom, liberty, justice, equal opportunity to use your talents to reach the full span of your potential, and so on and so forth. When your country tells you to dream and proceeds to build her institutions and civic processes around the enhancement of that national philosophy, you are ready to die for such a country. This explains the pervasive sense of civic struggle in America to retain the essence of that myth – the American dream.

What Americans call the American dream, the French refer to as *l'oeuvre nationale* or *l'oeuvre de la République*. These translate literally as 'national work' or 'the work of the Republic'. Unfortunately, there is an entire philosophical world lost in translation here. One needs to be French or immersed in French culture, language, history, and civilisation to fully grasp the centrality of *l'oeuvre nationale* as the fundamental and defining essence of the national project in France. Even a sleeping Frenchman could rationalise his sleep as part of *l'oeuvre nationale* because he is so completely defined by that ethos. In essence, this philosophy operates in France – and for the French – in much the same way as the American dream operates in America and for Americans: the sum of national beingness and aspiration. In some ways, *l'oeuvre nationale* even accounts for Gallic arrogance – that conviction on the part of your average French citizen that his or her language, culture, and civilisation are superior to those of every other European people. After all, the French say, we are the only ones who see those things as work and we have been at it since 1789!

Enter Nigeria. Enter Abuja. Welcome to the land of the national myth as appetiser! In fact, we don't even have a national myth, because what we have is so embarrassing it does not qualify to be labelled with the solemnity of a national myth. Where Americans have the American dream and the French have *l'oeuvre nationale*, we have 'the national cake' in Nigeria.

That is the operative national metaphor and one of the most evocative explanations of our national tragedy. It is the laziest, most unimaginative national myth I have ever encountered. If a country defines itself as a dream, that commands my civic attention because dreams are meant to be realised; if a country defines itself as work, that also retains my attention because I know what devolves from hard work; if, however, a country defines itself as dessert, and even proceeds to block the majority of its citizenry from that chocolate cake, I know that I have to cut corners to get my share of that cake after which I shit and it ends up as excreta. End of story. Our own national myth holds the key to corruption.

In essence, many aspects of our national malaise are tied to our loss of the struggle for meaning and there can be no respite until we understand the full ramifications of this phenomenon. Followership in Nigeria has been largely complicit in our losses in the field of meaning. We always wait for definitions to evolve from our contemptible ruling elite. The second phase emerges when the poltroons in the editorial rooms of the media regurgitate such brain-dead definitions of nation-ness. Phase three: we the people accept the nonsense defined for us and begin to struggle for crumbs. For instance, it is impossible to read a Nigerian newspaper without encountering that embarrassing phrase 'national cake'. If imbecilic rulers define Nigeria as consumption, must the media legitimise it through endless repetition and regurgitation? And what do we the people do? We accept Nigeria as national cake – which in fact means accepting defeat in the struggle for meaning – and proceed to devote strategic civic struggle to the creation of more states and local government areas to better access the national cake! Yet those who won the struggle to make Nigeria mean gorging and consumption cannot even produce a pin. We therefore have stupid rulers who define Nigeria as a cake but must import icing sugar, baking powder, and dessert plates and cutlery from China!

There is more. We the people made gradual concessions until we lost the struggle to define leadership. Like the definition of foundational myths, serious nations set considerable store by what they mean by leadership. To feed my mind, every day I read more than a dozen newspapers straddling Africa, Europe, the Americas, and Asia. One gets a sense of national and regional registers and diction from such an exercise. My assessment is that no other country in the world has as many 'leaders' as Nigeria. I encounter the word 'leader' so rarely in the world's newspapers that I have formed the impression that every country, except Nigeria, is miserly with that word. Go to a Nigerian newspaper and it is not unlikely for some foolish local government chairman from the Peoples Democratic Party to refer to himself as a 'leader'. Once he gets away with calling himself a leader, he will add 'chieftain' and 'stakeholder' to the tally in his next media interview. As usual, our newspapers legitimise such egregious abuses of the word by allowing it. Hence, the media and we the people reinforce that self-referential nonsense by creating a nation-space in which the likes of Ibrahim Babangida, Olusegun Obasanjo, James Ibori, Bukola Saraki, Andy Uba, Olabode George, Diepreye Alamieyeseigha, Atiku Abubakar, the clowns in the national and state assemblies, and everybody in the national secretariat of the PDP are free to call themselves leaders! We are lucky that Maurice Iwu is not yet calling himself a leader and stakeholder, but that won't be long in coming.

Our semantic concessions have consequences that are real and that impact on lives and national destiny. When the people lose the struggle to define leadership and determine its parameters, when the media and other agents of national meaning reinforce this loss by allowing every charlatan to refer to themselves as leaders and stakeholders on their pages, we pay a tremendous price in terms of how our society evolves.

For instance, we have produced a minimum of two generations of Nigerians for whom leadership essentially means the politics of the belly, spelt out in terms of the negative atmospherics of power – political office at all costs, convoys and sirens, and a vocabulary of civics lifted out of the pages of the training manual at the Nigerian Defence Academy. I have friends and relatives of my generation whose entire political phraseology is about which states or wards have been 'captured' or not captured by the PDP, which chieftain 'dealt ruthlessly' with which chieftain.

But we pay other prices. Often, those who participate in national discourse from the perspective of the singular importance of science and technology to national development – and the attendant need to focus our energies solely on the hard sciences and rubbish disciplines like history in our secondary schools – are not just contributing to the creation of a national attitude of condescension to 'non-scientific' areas of the national quest. They are also contributing to a culture of surrender of meaning by forgetting that science and technology have no meaning in the absence of the sort of visionary leadership that would translate such into concrete indices of progress in the lives of the people. Science and technology are managed by those who win the struggle for meaning. Where the people have lost the struggle for meaning and leadership is accessed and defined by charlatans, scientific breakthrough is like casting pearls before swine. Send Philip Emeagwali to Abuja and they may make him a Senior Special Adviser to the President on Tourism, Arts, and Culture. Send the famous historian Toyin Falola to Abuja and they may make him Minister of Health or Special Adviser to the President on Special Duties.

There is perhaps no better indication of the consequences of loss in the field of meaning than the recent collapse of the bid to secure voting rights for diasporic Nigerians. The commendable efforts of the leadership of diaspora Nigeria all came down to who gets to define meaning in Abuja – the meaning of citizenship. While those at the forefront of the struggle for diaspora voting rights got all their meanings right, those with the power to translate meaning into reality in Abuja clung to rebarbative understandings of civic inclusion as a function of residence and location. They put another nail in the coffin of meaning in Nigeria.

26

THE ENTOMBED: DOUBLE-CONSCIOUSNESS NIGERIANA

First, the grim description of someone familiar to most of us:

> Practically, this group imprisonment within a group has various effects upon the prisoner. He becomes provincial and centered upon the problems of his particular group. He tends to neglect the wider aspects of national life and human existence. On the other hand he is unselfish so far as his inner group is concerned. He thinks of himself not as an individual but as a group man, a 'race' man. His loyalty to this group idea tends to be almost unending and balks at almost no sacrifice. On the other hand, his attitude toward the environing race congeals into a matter of unreasoning resentment and even hatred, deep disbelief in them and refusal to conceive honesty and rational thought on their part. This attitude adds to the difficulties of conversation, intercourse, understanding between groups.

Next, a name for this racial and ethnic claustrophile. Finding 'prisoner' too generous a name, 'imprisonment' too mild a label for this existential condition, W.E.B. Du Bois calls the archetypal subject of his reflections above 'The Entombed'. Our friend, The Entombed, appears as a subject of reflection in *Dusk of Dawn*, a collection of autobiographical essays that Du Bois published in 1940, a full twenty years before Nigeria was born into conditions that predisposed her to become a mass producer of The Entombed. *Dusk of Dawn* also came some four decades after the publication of Du Bois's most famous book, *The Souls of Black Folk*, in which he proposed one of the most enduring theses on the black condition in America: double consciousness. Being Negro. Being American. Two antipodal conditions warring for the soul of a single subject. Striving to be both, Du Bois assures us, leads to existential anguish.

Strife is the keyword. Du Bois uses it frequently. His fecund mind and expansive writings prepared the philosophical basis for a lot of things. Things as disparate as the paths of Martin Luther King Jnr and Malcolm X. Things as improbable as giving us a window into double-consciousness Nigeriana: the wretched condition of Nigeria's vast tribe of The Entombed. Trust Nigeria: we added *maggi*, *ajinomoto*, *tatase*, and *tomapep* to Du Bois's original conceptualisation of double consciousness in order to make it Nigerian. For Du Bois, double consciousness implies the historical struggle to merge the Negro and the American into one 'truer' holistic self in which neither of the selves would disappear. For Du Bois, while these two selves may have been historically conditioned to be hostile to each other, they are not mutually exclusive or irreconcilable.

For The Entombed in Nigeria, double consciousness is not a striving to be Nigerian and Yoruba, Nigerian and Igbo, Nigerian and Hausa, Nigerian and Edo, Nigerian and Ogoni. Double-consciousness Nigeriana is part affirmation, part negation. It is the perpetual war and strife to be Igbo and not Nigerian, Yoruba and not Nigerian, Ijaw and not Nigerian. This civil war between affirmation of the ethno and negation of the national defines the life and reality of The Entombed in Nigeria.

The Entombed arrived at his current existential impasse through a tragic misreading of our collective and justified dissatisfaction with and rejection of the nature and character of the Nigerian state and her visionless and corrupt rulers as an end in itself. The truly uplifting, challenging, but cerebrally taxing responsibility is to use discontent with Project Nigeria as the basis of envisioning and working for an alternative and very possible new Nigeria, shorn of the buffooneries of the buccaneers in charge of our national destiny in Abuja. Discontent with and uncompromising rejection of the order we have had since independence should be the basis of a sustained struggle to take Nigeria back from the looters and rebuild her on a foundation of fairness and justice. Precisely because this task is mentally demanding, The Entombed takes the lazier route of discontent as an end in itself, avoids vision and the profundity of thought it requires, and locks himself up in the airless urn of misinterpreted or over-interpreted ethnicity.

Why would Du Bois invent a carceral metaphor of death for this character? Why The Entombed? The answer lies in the atrocious psychology of this Nigerian. Within the dynamics of our national experience, The Entombed is dead. Dead to the humanity of the Others he manufactures prodigiously and robotically in every Nigerian ethnic group that is not his own. Dead to the intrinsic humanism of his own culture. While Du Bois's double consciousness is resolved in favour of life and the overcoming of adversity to embrace the humanity of the Other, double-consciousness Nigeriana embraces death as resolution. Its cogito is strange: I am Igbo/Yoruba/Hausa/Edo/Idoma/Ijaw, *therefore you are not human*. At this point, we are less than a kilometre away from Wole Soyinka's grim rendition of the final destination of such absolutisms: I am right, therefore you are dead!

Hate is the pounded yam of The Entombed in Nigeria. Locked in a tragic misapprehension of his own culture and deaf to everything his ethnicity teaches him about humanism, he clings to robotic, gratuitous hatred of the Other as evidence of his new status as the Praetorian Guard of his ethnic group. Behold the self-appointed champion of puritanical Igboness! Behold the delusional defender of hermetic Yorubaness! Behold the jihadic gatekeeper of fundamentalist Hausa-Fulaniness! All that is left now is to equip his tongue with the most purulent, hate-filled vocabulary ever known to man for woolly-headed deployment in his daily engagements with Nigerian humanity outside of his ethnic group.

I have a name for the language of the Nigerian Entombed. I call it *gutterlect*. This hare-brained character uses such hideous gutterlect in blanket descriptions of Nigerians outside of his ethnic group as would make Eugene Terre'Blanche cringe at the thought of using such language for the kaffirs who continue to haunt his soul in South Africa. Needless to say, the Nigerian Entombed is strictly monolingual. He speaks only gutterlect. If this character is based in Nigeria, he stops at being just an atrocious member of the human race. If he is based in the diaspora, especially in the West, he combines what discredited French philosopher Lucien Lévy-Bruhl calls 'pre-logical mentality' with the atrociousness of his Nigeria-based cousin.

If you frequent Nigerian e-sites and listservs in search of serious kindred minds committed to channelling their non-negotiable and total rejection of Nigeria as is towards the envisioning of a possible and alternative Nigeria, you have most certainly encountered The Entombed and his gutterlect of hate. No Nigerian ethnic group enjoys a monopoly. They all contribute their share to the e-pool of The Entombed. The differences lie in the quality of the minds. Hence, The Entombed may be a university professor from whom much better is expected but who finds time to exchange endless ethnicist taunts, jabs, and trivia with folks below his station; he may be a lawyer, an architect, a medical doctor; or he may be a truculent rabble-rouser who is unable to put together a single grammatical sentence in English. No matter the differences in intellectual depth, gutterlect and programmatic blindness to the humanity of the Other unite them all. Sanusi Lamido Sanusi? That sounds Hausa-Fulani, isn't it? He is not Igbo? Not Yoruba? Not even a south-southerner? A scholar of Islam to boot! How dare he? And how is it even imaginable that 'this Taliban' could possess any modicum of rational thought, let alone head the Central Bank? I must hurry to hate him at once. I must 'hurry him down to the grave', as the poet Ogaga Ifowodo would put it. I'll fish for reasons later.

Never mind that this puny hater and gutterlecter cannot hold a candle to Sanusi Lamido Sanusi's considerable achievements in matters cerebral. The important thing is that this lion (The Entombed) must have that antelope (Sanusi Lamido Sanusi) for dinner because, in the nature of things in Nigeria, guilt is always ethnically predetermined. My grandmother's tales by moonlight attest to that. 'Ah, you this stupid antelope (*iwo agbonrin buruku yi*), I have caught you today! You are the one who insulted me yesterday,' roars the lion. Replies the frightened antelope: 'Ah, you must be mistaking me for someone else, sir. I wasn't even here yesterday. I was out of town.' 'Shut up my friend! That's how you insulted me last year!' roars the furious lion. The antelope replies, 'Last year? But I was born this year, sir!' 'Ehen, are you trying to say that I am lying? Go ahead and kuku call me a liar. That's how your mother insulted me this morning.' 'But my mother died last year, sir!' 'Shut your fucking mouth! If it wasn't your mother who insulted me, it was surely your father or some other relative of yours.' If the lion keeps fishing, as he surely will, one reason will eventually stick as justification for hate.

So what exactly is our entombed gutter-mouth missing in

his culture as he stands sentinel at the gate of ethnos, keeping the humanity of the Other at bay? He misses the fact that the good Nigerian must begin by being a ferociously good Yoruba or Igbo. The ferociously good Yoruba or Igbo, in turn, understands that his culture is not a blanket manifesto of hate. He has the allegorical evidence of some of the greatest narratives in his culture to lead him to this conclusion about the fate of the absolutist and delusional gatekeeper. If only he knows how to read! Consider the allegorical adventure of Olowo Aiye, the brave hunter in D.O. Fagunwa's *Igbo Olodumare* who ventures out of the familiar to encounter the Other. He must meet other members of the human species as well as creatures of the chthonic realm in this fascinating enactment of the quest motif. Between Olowo Aiye and the experience of humane and enriching contact with Otherness stands Anjonu Iberu, literally 'the *ghomid* of fear'.

Anjonu Iberu stands sentinel at the gates of the forest to purvey hate and keep the Other at bay. He is truly fearful, oozing fire and heavy smoke from a hole at the centre of his head. He singularly and tyrannically determines who belongs in and who belongs out. He is the father of our modern-day sentinels and defenders of ethnic fundamentalism in Nigeria. He is an absolutist who traffics in gutterlect like his children who now prowl e-Nigeria. In the end, the cosmopolitanism and boundless humanism of Olowo Aiye crushes the absolutism of the entombed Anjonu Iberu. Alas, our Yoruba gutterlecters do not know how to read Anjonu Iberu as an allegory of absolutism. *Igbo Olodumare* was published in 1949. Nine years later, another absolutist gatekeeper and atrocious misreader of his culture makes a grand allegorical entry into posterity as Africa's most famous narrative character. His name is Okonkwo, the Ogbuefi who has to be more Igbo than every other Igbo in Umuofia and the surrounding villages, defending his culture by breaking every rule of the said culture through brash over-interpretation and perpetual misreading. Like Anjonu Iberu, his textual brother by nine years, we know where and how Okonkwo ends. Alas, our Igbo gutterlecters do not know how to read Okonkwo as an allegory of absolutism.

Because the members of Nigeria's Entombed People's Party have considerable trouble with reading comprehension and it is their wont to misunderstand and dis-understand everything they read, we must remind them that there is something they are missing in the thought and oeuvre of Nigeria's most humanised, most uncompromisable thinkers in the progressive column of history. Take a nuanced look at the thought and praxis of non-entombed progressive thinkers and activists like Wole Soyinka, Gani Fawehinmi, Okey Ndibe, Femi Falana, Bamidele Aturu, Ayo Obe, Omoyele Sowore, the late Chuma Ubani, and Abayomi Ferreira and you will notice a common premise: *a total, uncompromising, and categorical rejection of a certain version of Nigeria*. That version of Nigeria, evidenced by the gluttonous and prebendal instincts of our pernicious rulers, must die in order for a genuine Nigeria to emerge and acquire a salutary space under the sun. Nowhere in the thought and praxis of these men and women would you find the sort of dead-endist ethnic claustrophilia that powers the little world of The Entombed. The double-consciousness Nigeriana of a Wole Soyinka or an Okey Ndibe is not one that finds resolution in being dead to the humanity of the Other Nigerian.

To transform our complete rejection of Nigeria as is (that Nigeria that is Polyphemus) to an end in itself – as The Entombed folks rabble-rousing in Internet forums are doing – rather than make it the basis of a sustained struggle for a Nigerian renaissance is to concede for another sixty years the last word on Nigeria to President Yar'Adua, Atiku Abubakar, David Mark, Olusegun Obasanjo, Ibrahim Babangida, James Ibori, Peter Odili, Lucky Igbinedion, Bukola Saraki, Olabode George, Dimeji Bankole, Andy Uba, Vincent Ogbulafor,

Ahmadu Alli, Tony Anenih, and all other members of this dangerous and unholy tribe who have arrogantly assured us of the perennity of their wicked version of Nigeria. It is to claim that after these dangerous people, it is smithereens. That isn't even an option we should entertain. In the end, *kangun kangun kangun a kangun sibi kan* (what will be will be). There are three choices, three Nigerias, and only one will prevail: the Nigeria of the looters listed above, the non-Nigeria of The Entombed that hates and despises robotically on the basis of ethnicity, and the Nigeria of the dreams of our progressive activists and heroes. Come the day of the last version!

27

PROJECT NIGERIA: VIATICUM FOR POLYPHEMUS

The current condition of statehood in Nigeria calls to mind two seemingly far-flung and historically divergent analogies, one rooted in the Roman Catholic rites of passage for the dying and the other lodged in the fate that awaits anyone who stands in the path of freedom and justice in Greek mythology. The analogies shall remain, I hope, only tentatively far-flung and divergent as I weave them into a workable allegory of the Nigerian condition in the light of President Yar'Adua's ongoing festival of murder in the Niger Delta. Viaticum, the Eucharist or last communion administered to the dying in the Catholic tradition, has been made familiar to Nigerians of a certain generation by the Senegalese poet Birago Diop. Those who went to secondary school when Nigeria still had an education sector worthy of that name will remember Birago Diop's poem 'Viaticum', an Africanised, mytho-ritualistic rendering of that Catholic rite as a passage to life in the shadow of the breath of the ancestors. Diop's 'Viaticum' was included in Donatus

Nwoga's *West African Verse* in order to introduce anglophone audiences to African writing in French.

The ancient Greeks imagined Polyphemus as a one-eyed Cyclops who trapped Odysseus and his men in his cave during their journey home from the Trojan War. Polyphemus had plenty of common sense before the homeward-bound Greeks got trapped in his cave. That singular development led to a lot of things that would affect the entire history of narration and human imagination from Homer through Ovid to our times. For our purposes here, it is sufficient to recall that the presence of the Greek hostages in his cave marked the moment of transition to a pathology of food and consumption in the psyche of Polyphemus. Drooling at the prospect of gorging, Polyphemus redefined the entire atmospherics in his cave around that primal instinct: food, gorging, and the politics of the belly. Exit common sense. Exit fairness. Exit justice. One or two entrapped Greeks for dinner, some wine, then sleep, and another one or two Greeks for breakfast before taking his sheep out to graze. That became the bacchanal clockwork of Polyphemus's life until Odysseus and his men taught him a vital lesson: the desire for freedom is the only food that nourishes the human spirit. Not even a one-eyed cannibalistic Cyclops, with all the legitimate and illegitimate apparatuses of power and violence in his possession, could kill the spirit of freedom. That spirit defeated him. It was predictable.

For me, the moment Polyphemus redefined the meaning of his cave as food upon discovery of the trapped Greek travellers is also the very moment that he became the direct ancestor of the Nigerian state and the scrofulous characters who constitute its rulership at all three levels of normative misgovernance. The parallels are too obvious and tempting. Witness the behaviour of this state since it struck oil in the Niger Delta. The fruit of rulership in Nigeria has never been able to fall far from the tree of Polyphemus. The Greek monster discovered food in his cave, lost common sense, and redefined his territory and entire world around food and gorging. Nigeria's rulers and the Nigerian state discovered oil in the Niger Delta, lost common sense, and redefined Nigeria and the Nigerian state around food and gorging. Anyone minimally familiar with the story of Polyphemus and his behaviour at the mere thought of losing that source of food and gorging which had become the very basis of his ontology will have no trouble understanding the unbelievable imbecilities of the Nigerian state in terms of her handling of the food cave that is the Niger Delta. Even the renewed viciousness and murderousness – in fact, state terrorism – that we are currently witnessing have perfectly logical explanations in the trough of the Polyphemus narrative: the closer the monster got to a sense of the imminence of the end of his stabilised order of food and gorging, the madder and more vicious he became.

At no other time have Nigeria's thieving rulers felt such a compelling imminence of the beginning of the end of a predatory order that one of them, chieftain and stakeholder Vincent Ogbulafor, reminded us recently would last another sixty years. At the level of international symbolism, they are finally beginning to wake up to the fact that the despicable system they run has transformed them into a continental open sore that everyone – except the truly inconsequential – now avoids. They lobbied for a state visit to Washington by President Yar'Adua. No luck. The G20 poured cold water on them. FIFA is also now diplomatically rubbing their incompetence in their noses. Not content with predicting the implosion of Nigeria, the American state has now made a loud statement with President Obama's first trip to Africa. Nigeria is left to hosting an inconsequential French prime minister and President Faure Gnassingbe of Togo, who even allowed himself the indulgence of having ideas on what we could do to improve ourselves! When you are felled by a macro-indignity, you become the foot mat of all sorts of micro-indignities. When South Africa, Ghana,

Botswana, Namibia, and even the Benin Republic become the leaders of the continent, and Nigeria is reduced to receiving advice from the thirty-something-year-old son of Gnassingbé Eyadéma who, but for the accident of his birth, should still be writing and submitting term papers in a graduate programme here in the West, you know that we are truly finished. Next, Blaise Compaoré's daughter will have ideas on how to move Nigeria forward. Unfortunately, no dictionary in Aso Rock has an entry for shame.

The dwindling fortune of oil in global geopolitics and the international economy is another reason for the renewed desperation of Nigeria's rulers. Finally, this visionless class is waking up to the fact that the cookie jar has lost considerable value. The crash in the value of oil has considerably affected what is available to humour their gargantuan appetite. Simply put, oil is no longer fetching the kind of money that these guys are used to stealing. Green is in big time all over the world. President Obama takes independence from oil as seriously as the founding fathers of his country took independence from Britain. A significant number of the oil states in the Arabian Gulf are now only oil states in name. They have diversified massively into non-oil-sector mega-earning. Dubai is buying up everything in the West and transforming itself into the world's number one tourist destination to secure non-oil earnings. Every Nigerian should make it a habit to read daily at least one online English-language newspaper from countries like Kuwait, Oman, Saudi Arabia, and the United Arab Emirates. Read their financial/economy pages, a treasure trove of information on the giant strides they have made to free their national budgets of oil dependency, and you will feel truly sorry for Nigeria. You will wonder how cerebral conservative Muslims are building some of the world's most amazing postmodern societies while Nigeria's conservative northern Muslims can only boast a paltry legacy of selective sharia for the poor after decades of chokehold on federal power and oil money.

The imminence of a new post-oil global order has caught Nigeria's unimaginative rulers with their pants down. Too busy gorging on easy money and easy food, our Ali Babas in Abuja never envisaged the current threat to oil and are too intellectually lazy to begin to envision post-oil national budgets this late in the day. Here is a ruling class that couldn't even envisage post-war Angola as the end of Nigeria's continental oil dominance and plan strategically for it. Non-oil earning also implies the sort of hard work, planning, and execution that has never been the forte of this class of indolent rulers. With oil, all you really need to do is sit down in government guest chalets in Abuja and award oil blocks over pepper soup and easy women while waiting for rent and bribes to pour into your onshore and offshore accounts from Shell, ChevronTexaco, Julius Berger, and other Western 419 multinationals. Consequently, the only strategy that the cerebral limitations of the Nigerian ruling class allow for is to increase the tempo and scale of the gorging while the party lasts, hence the need to clamp down viciously on militants – even if it means exterminating the entire civilian population of the Niger Delta in the process.

The tragedy in the Niger Delta has, sadly, brought out the beast in us and our polity. In the absence of a formally declared state of war, a civilian president orders air raids and bombings of civilians in broad daylight – a violation of our collective humanity that not even our worst and most vicious military despoilers ever imagined – and there is no national uprising. We had somehow naively believed that we couldn't possibly experience anything worse than the spectacle of General Sani Abacha's tanks in Lagos. What exactly will it take for Nigerians to rise up and drive these crazy baldheads out of town? Add mustard and serum gas to President Yar'Adua's pacification of his own people and you get Saddam Hussein. Surely the Mullah of Katsina is methodically applying everything he read in the *Handbook on the Pacification of the Primitive Tribes of the Middle Belt and the Niger Delta by the Nigerian State*.

Rather than take the full measure of President Yar'Adua's unbelievable crimes against humanity and begin to work to ensure that he gets the Omar Bashir treatment before or after he leaves office, we have a divided commentariat, with some preferring to focus on the criminality of the militants and the right of the Nigerian state to defend itself as the only legitimate repository of the instruments of violence and the only entity vested with the right to discipline and punish. As if history avails them of any freedom struggle that does not produce sanguinary and selfish criminals who could potentially undermine and derail the cause. This, of course, does not justify the criminality of the militants, but to focus on that and ignore the catalytic criminality of the Nigerian state is beyond me. The high point of these vacuous forays into Political Science 101 came from a Nigerian doctoral student in Germany who recently published an apologia for President Yar'Adua in *The Guardian*. What these emergency aficionados of political science and theories of the prerogatives of the Westphalian state fail to tell us is that the rights of the state to legitimate violence are predicated on numerous obligations to the citizen in the context of the social contract. I have written elsewhere that the Nigerian state cannot be accused, even by her most generous defenders, of having the slightest understanding of her obligations to her citizens. She does not guarantee their security and their right to the pursuit of happiness. She does not guarantee their right to life and human dignity. When they are dead, she leaves them to rot in the streets.

Where the state meets her obligations to us as citizens, we all agree to submit ourselves voluntarily to her regime of discipline and punish. This is where the state derives her hegemony from: our voluntary submission to her authority because she is meeting her own part of the deal. Absent this, enter 'dominance without hegemony', a concept made famous by Ranajit Guha, one of India's most prominent historians, in his masterful work on colonialism. Guha owes his thought on hegemony to the famous Italian Marxist thinker Antonio Gramsci. The colonial state, Guha argues, had dominance because it successfully enforced its structures, institutions, and regimes of violence on the people, but she lacked hegemony because the people never willingly surrendered their subjecthood to her nor did they ever recognise her as the repository of legitimate violence. Anyone recognise the Nigerian state in this description? The Nigerian state, embodied in the federal government of Nigeria, is one of the best postcolonial illustrations of Ranajit Guha's dominance without hegemony in Africa. Because it is in the hands of the most venal characters we have to offer, and who get there only by rigging or plotting coups, our state does not command the loyalty of the people. Our state exists mainly in a relationship of force and violence with the citizenry, having legitimacy and hegemony only with those who are gorging: less than one per cent of all 150 million of us.

To concede the right to pacificatory and legitimate violence to a state that is one hundred per cent dominance and zero per cent hegemony as some commentators have been doing beats me. It betrays their poor reading of history. Worse are the commentators who bring ethnicism to the table. Good for those Niger Deltans! They did not support Biafra. Considerable strategic thought is then wasted on the intermesh – or lack thereof – of Biafra and the Niger Delta struggle. Those who are taking their eyes off the ball of genocide in the Niger Delta assume that the discourse and history of secession in Nigeria are tied singularly to Biafra. As early as 1964, Isaac Sha'ahu of the University of Maryland, Baltimore County, had threatened in the Northern House of Assembly that the Tivs would 'pull out of the North and the Federation as a whole. We shall be a sovereign state, we shall be joining nobody. We are 1 000 000 in population, bigger than Gambia and Mauritania.' Two years later, on 23 February 1966, Isaac Boro seceded and declared his Niger Delta People's Republic. Boro's new 'country' lasted a total of twelve days.

Although Boro declared his Republic in response to his and his people's perceived Igbo domination of eastern minorities, the broader point I want to make is that it is intellectually dishonest to claim that Biafra and the Niger Delta struggle are not interlinked. It is equally specious to claim that the people of the Niger Delta should somehow have preferred what they felt would be domination in Biafra to domination in Nigeria. It is like asking Cameroonians if they preferred French to German colonialism. As an outsider to both struggles who must reflect on them with humility, what I see are two histories of oppression and two struggles against the injustices of the Nigerian arrangement that are being weakened by the divide-and-rule strategies of the centre. Let's keep the Igbos and the Niger Deltans busy arguing over who is more victim and who betrayed whom in order to better exploit and marginalise both of them. That strategy works and has served the Nigerian state very well.

Biafra sits at the heart of a long history of discontent with and resistance against the myriad injustices of the Nigerian arrangement. Because it is the only discontent with Project Nigeria that led to a civil war and more than a million dead, it has become the grand organising metaphor of all other localised discontents with Project Nigeria. Biafra and the Niger Delta – as indeed all other agitations such as the increasingly loud calls for a possible Oodua Republic – form a continuum of discontent with Project Nigeria and we must engage them as such while respecting the singular circumstances and the ethno-localised integrity of each struggle. Biafra also provides the pathway for hope that Polyphemus will never defeat the spirit of freedom at the core of the agitations in the Niger Delta.

Freedom is spirit. Freedom is a way of being. A way of being certain that Polyphemus represents your Absolute Negation and you can only genuinely *be* when you negate that Absolute Negation through a process Frantz Fanon calls therapeutic violence. This dialectic explains why a traumatic war, permanent exclusion from the presidency, and the periodic slaughter of the Igbo in the north have never uprooted a single hair from the head of Biafra. Biafra is spirit. Biafra is identitarian immanence. So also is the Niger Delta. That struggle too is spirit. Every struggle for freedom by any oppressed nationality in Nigeria is spirit and immanence. President Yar'Adua's bombs will stop nothing in the Niger Delta. I feel so sorry for him. He is a university professor and should ordinarily have no trouble understanding this but Polyphemus is too set in his predictable ways.

I wager that nobody in Abuja has any doubt that we are beginning to approach the end of the road for Polyphemus. There can be no doubt in the minds of our enemies that they cannot sustain the monumental injustice that is currently Nigeria for much longer – hence the viciousness and the need to acquire more before the cookie crumbles. The Niger Delta is their last vicious throe. Their road map going forward is predictable. They will leave the Niger Delta desolate after the current orgy of blood to prepare the next orgy: the elections of 2011. This is when, hopefully, they will kill and rig their way to implosion. As the Yoruba put it, those who eat *gbi* will surely die *gbi*. Polyphemus is now on an inexorable course to dying *gbi* in Nigeria. This thieving, murdering, and gorging Polyphemus must die for the Nigeria of our dreams, hopes, and aspirations to emerge. For me, freedom is not the disintegration of Nigeria but the annihilation of the system that has held Nigeria and Nigerians in bondage for so long and has refused to let us renegotiate the terms of engagement. That system is Polyphemus and I am glad to be present at her viaticum.

28

ORILE EDE

Orile ede is the Yoruba expression for the cluster of nation/ state/country. Basil Davidson, one of my favourite chroniclers of Africa, famously declared the African nation-state a curse. Davidson was coming from the overwhelming evidence of the failure of the state in Africa. Long before him, Obafemi Awolowo, in totally different circumstances, declared Nigeria 'a mere geographical expression', empty of many of the conditions that Ernest Renan, the famous nineteenth-century French philosopher, assures us must be assembled before we can speak of a nation. Awolowo's became a prophetic phrase that subsequently found immense currency and fortune as the unlucky Nigerian state fell into the hands of successive generations of some of Africa's most talented buccaneers. In fact, to declare the African nation-state a curse in the presence of a Nigerian is to make him experience the uncomfortable itch of an old woman in whose presence dry bones are being mocked. Apologies to Chinua Achebe and the Igbo owners of that proverb.

Whenever I'm invited to reflect critically on the condition of the state in Africa using Nigeria as an example, I always love to unpack the philosophical underpinnings of *orile ede*, if only to illustrate how and why Nigeria's project nationhood was doomed from the very beginning and why we need to revisit those beginnings, and correct so many errors of the rendering, if we are to stand any chance of renegotiating our way out of the current stasis to genuine nationhood. My strategy obviously carries the risk of assuming that what is valid in/for the Yoruba world is valid in/for the rest of Nigeria and Africa. I do not necessarily want to echo Wole Soyinka whose 'African World' in *Myth, Literature, and the African World* is largely a Yoruba world.

The risk, I believe, is worth taking. All you need do is reflect on your own African mother tongue to determine if it is embarrassed by the same conceptual dilemmas in the attempt to imagine and name the modern concepts of nation, state, and country. I intend this as a template upon which any African could try to inscribe cultural imaginings of the nation-state in his/her own language. *Orile ede*, again, is how the Yoruba express the geographical and political categories of country, nation, and state. Hence, *orile ede Naijeria* literally means 'the land of the language of Nigeria'. If you insist on a further breakdown, you end up with 'the head, land, and language of Nigeria'. This is the first sign of trouble. There is a conceptual dissonance between two orders of apprehension, the one Western and the other Yoruba. Being a civilisation of the verb, the Yoruba have no use for the restrictive lexical and conceptual economy of European civilisation – hence three major elements of Yoruba cosmogony, each worth several doctoral dissertations, are packed into *orile ede*.

If the *orile* part of the business stopped at just meaning 'chief-land', 'head-land', 'origin-land', or 'source-land', our trouble would be considerably reduced even if not altogether eliminated. But logged in the profoundest semantic recesses of *orile* in the Yoruba world are aspects of *ori*, which means 'head' in the deep African sense of that word. 'Head' is not just the physical locus of the face, skull, and brain that we carry around. 'Head' is at once the expression of origins, fate, and destiny. It authenticates the Yoruba being in its marriage or contact with the earth, hence its ecumenical unity with *ile* in *orile*. For the Yoruba subject, to declare that 'my head touched the earth' in this town or on this soil is the ultimate pact of origin. If you want to really kill the soul of a Yoruba man, tell him that he or his fathers 'walked to their hometown on their legs, not on their heads'. You just called him a bastard. This explains why the *oriki orile*, associated with the praise of sources, origins, and beginnings, is one of the most important aspects of the *oriki* genre. Significant verses in my family's/clan's *oriki orile* continuously evoke the intermingling of 'head' and 'land' in the historical trajectory of my people.

Chinua Achebe makes it easy to translate this 'head' for the non-Yoruba and non-Africans. The Yoruba *ori* is a rough equivalent of the Igbo *chi*. If you were translating *Things Fall Apart* into Yoruba, you would have to use *ori* everywhere Achebe uses *chi* in the novel. I will therefore use *ori* and *chi* interchangeably in this discussion to remind non-African readers of the pertinence of Achebe's rendering of things to my purposes here, while mindful of the ethno-cultural specificity of each. The *ile* part of the equation in *orile* is just as problematic. *Ile* means 'land' in all its African psychic and chthonic dimensions that European languages are not equipped to carry. For instance, there is no proper rendition in English of the expression *ile Yoruba*. All you have are paltry consolations such as 'the land of the Yoruba', 'the territory of the Yoruba', or the more common 'Yoruba land'. There is an entire world lost in translation here. Finally there is *ede*, which means 'language'. In essence, a country/state/nation needs *ori* (head), *ile* (land),

and *ede* (language) – all in the African sense – for that Western reality *to be* in Yoruba.

Let's start with the enormous problems posed by *ori*. Now I do not speak Igbo. But let's assume for the sake of argument that the Igbo idea of country/state/nation also contains *chi*. That would mean that Nigeria as a geopolitical entity has a *chi*. Were this the case in Igbo, as it most certainly is in Yoruba, the first question any serious Igbo should ask instinctively is, who owns this *chi*? The Ashanti should ask the same question if, like the golden stool, their idea of Ghana contains aspects of *sumsum* (soul). I ask myself that question all the time: who owns that *ori* in *orile ede Naijeria*? The answer is as unpleasant as it is unacceptable: a murderous Hausa-Fulani establishment, aided by Yoruba, Igbo, and other ethnic minority bellhops like Goodluck Jonathan, has owned Nigeria's *ori* since 1960.

Now we all know how extremely personal the *ori* – and its equivalents all over Africa – is to our people. So, who among Nigeria's three hundred or so fiercely independent ethnic nationalities is willing to dissolve their group's *ori* into a political contraption manufactured by Englishmen for the economic benefit of one parasitic queen? And how were those poor fools from England to know that beyond territory and resources, what they were actually trying to do was to weld more than three hundred *oris* or *chis* together in a single political union? A recipe for total disaster. Has anyone ever heard of a marriage of *oris*? Even in the context of a traditional conjugal union between man and woman, each retains his or her individual *ori*; hence the Yoruba proverb *Ile aiye l'a pade, ototo l'a rin wa* (Earth is just a common meeting point, we all came through different predestinations).

The trouble with land is self-explanatory so I will move on to *ede* – language. Implicit in the Yoruba rendering of country/ nation/state is that the said political entity has a language. Ironically, the Yoruba are even better equipped to describe that reality when it applies to Europeans. The French have no profounder way of naming and calling their country than France. For the Yoruba, it is *orile ede Faranse*, which would translate roughly as 'the head, the land, and the language of France' or 'the land of the language of France'. The Yoruba rendering is immensely richer than what any French national could ever come up with. But that is possible because France has one language that commands the loyalty of all French nationals as the bearer of their identity, history, culture, and civilisation. Even where you have separatist tendencies as in Corsica, we must bear in mind that the Corsicans are only fighting for their own separate *ori*, not their own separate language. No one is contesting the finality of French. As a nationalist rallying cry, 'Our ancestors the Gauls' will always be in business in France.

Shift the discourse to Nigeria and the problem becomes immediately obvious. Which *ede* do the Yoruba have in mind when they say *orile ede Naijeria*? I have shocked so many Yoruba interlocutors with this question because it has simply never occurred to them to think about Nigeria from that perspective. Again, which *ede*? Nigeria does not have a language. There are more than two hundred warring languages – many more if you consider dialectal variants – whose petty squabbles are arbitrated by one language: English. For obvious reasons, English does not command anyone's affective loyalty in Nigeria. The Yoruba have no concept of a country/state/nation without an *ede*, yet Nigeria has no *ede Nigeria* in that collective sense that the reality of nationhood requires in Yoruba. Only the ethnic entities within it have their respective *edes*. South Africa has tried to resolve this conceptual dissonance by recognising eleven official languages, but anyone who even remotely suggests that for Nigeria is looking for Rwanda and Darfur combined.

If this Yoruba example is anything to go by, the conclusion to be drawn is that Nigeria is a foreign mirage not easily transposable into the psychic and cognitive world of Yorunaija people. Nigeria as is does not represent anything that the Yoruba call *orile ede*! The nation-state has worked in the West largely because it requires only your submission to the absolute authority of its cartography, national myths, real or invented pasts, a collective present, a common destiny, the envisionment of a collective future, and, above all, the production of native Others. In Africa, the nation-state demands a lot more than these elements, as I have tried to show with the example of the Yoruba. It demands the sublimation of your *ori*, *ile*, *ede* within the unifying logic of a foreign political concept. This is where the ship of Benedict Anderson sinks on contact with the iceberg of Africa. Nigeria is the imagined community of whose *ori*? Of which and whose *ede*? Of whose *chi*? Ghana is the imagined community of whose *sumsum*?

Now the components of o*rile ede* as I have described them are not things you ask an African to surrender for any higher, collective purpose. Let me remind you that whatever the state takes from the citizen in the West, it gives back a lot more in terms of the rights and guarantees of citizenship under a democratic dispensation: the right to life, dignity, security, and the pursuit of happiness. In essence, there is a trade-off that demands a lot more from the state for the minimal conditions of the social contract to be met. I do not need to belabour the fact that Nigeria is a career defaulter that cannot be accused of possessing even the most rudimentary understanding of her obligations to the citizen under the social contract. We all know that. The unserious rebranders in Abuja and the rabid servicers of their illusions in the diaspora know that.

In essence, I am saying that I find all the contemporary explanations – especially in the social sciences – of the atrophy of project nationhood in Nigeria utterly unsatisfactory. The failure of the Nigerian state is too often tied to measurable corruption indices, failed state institutions, poverty, military intervention in politics, neocolonialism, and neoliberal propositions on how multinational and transnational globalisation and corporatism have weakened the state in Africa. These are all secondary explanations. As useful as I find them, Immanuel Wallerstein, Ernest Renan, Ernest Gellner, Benedict Anderson, and Masao Miyoshi are not sufficient to account for these things. The state failed in Nigeria because it was never able to harness the psychic, cultural, and chthonic predispositions it met on the ground to begin with. In fact, its Western arrogance and conceit made it dismiss those things as superstition. Can anybody imagine Lord Lugard calling a meeting of district officers to ruminate on how the protectorates and colony he amalgamated into a state would negotiate such concepts as *chi*, *ile*, and *ede* and make them workable within the dynamics of the state? Today, rather than return to and seek to understand these things in preparation for the future of Nigeria, there are still 'sophisticated' and 'postmodern' Nigerians prowling America, calling on us to grow and mature out of our ethnicities. Such is the tragedy!

Deep down in the Yoruba psyche, Nigeria will always be that strange and dubious Western entity asking for the surrender of your *ori*, *ile*, and *ede* without giving anything in return. I am assuming variations of this interpretation to be true to some extent for all or most of the constituent ethnic groups in Nigeria. I do not know any Igbo that would surrender his/her *chi* to something as factitious as Project Nigeria, a project they even deem genocidal in the first place. I will not talk about our folks from Ogoni, Odi, Zaki-Biam, and Agge. One would insult them by even asking them what they think of Project Nigeria! Resentment of Project Nigeria by the majority of her citizens – those who are 'eating' do not resent anything – therefore goes beyond competition for and access to resources, injustice, and the other usual explanations.

These are the cultural troughs we need to revisit in the

context of an open dialogue to renegotiate the terms of our national coexistence. Project Nigeria does not stand a chance if we continue to allow the selfish traducers of our destiny to block these discussions. The rulers (I refuse to call them leaders) who deceive themselves in Abuja that these questions are no-go areas while mouthing useless platitudes about the non-negotiability of the 'corporate existence of Nigeria' are not just blind to history because blindness sails their greedy boats. Tragically, they are tone-deaf to the memories logged in their cultures. Otherwise they would understand that there can be no finality over the making and remaking of project nation-state, a project which Ngugi wa Thiong'o reminds us is indicative of 'the planting of European memory in Africa'.

If by its nature this planted European memory requires me to surrender my *ori* as a precondition for its very existence, you cannot outlaw negotiation and continuous renegotiation of the terms of engagement. What does the future hold should the rapinous status quoists in Abuja and their voluntary megaphones in the diaspora continue their macabre dance on the grave of our hopes and aspirations as a people? The answer, my friends, is not blowing in the wind.

29

THE MYTH OF THE
GOOD YORUBA

In the postcolonial and cultural theory part of my work, I teach something called the 'production of otherness' at the graduate level. It has to do with how people, voices, or forces who perceive themselves as normative at certain points in history have represented those who do not look like them as anomalous, primitive, and inferior. Those producing 'the Other' always see themselves as the norm. In postcolonial theory, we call them 'the self'. For much of the last six hundred years, for instance, the white race has been the most active producer of otherness, operating as a self that represents all other races – especially the black race – as its inferior Others. Everywhere you turn to in human history, you encounter the phenomenon of otherness production. The self needs and breeds otherness in order to have value or even to exist. For instance, to satisfy that necessity, apartheid produced the kaffir; Islam produced the infidel; Christianity produced the unbeliever; heterosexuality produced the fag; Israelis produced the Araboushim; Americans produced the nigga; European colonisers produced the native; patriarchal man produced the hysteric woman. Even in Nigeria, the nightmare known as the Peoples Democratic Party is a self actively producing and victimising otherness: the Other of the PDP is otherwise known as the ordinary Nigerian.

Those who produce otherness always feel compelled to manufacture and acknowledge the rare exception, who is then severed from his source and hoisted as a trophy on a pedestal. The production of otherness is a process that does not tolerate things in the singular. Rather, it always strives to be a broad, all-encompassing basket into which the othered is dropped and stereotyped. Hence, all the negative traits that dominant white America churns out while othering the 'nigga' or the Native American are not designed to describe just one 'nigga' or one Indian. *Niggas are all like that. Indians are generally lazy. Kaffirs are thieves. Africans are all diseased and poverty-stricken. The Araboushim are all terrorists who want to destroy Israel. My broda take am easy. Shebi you know women, they are all like that jare.* The list of blanket stereotyping is endless in the production of otherness. The self that produces the Other possesses a tongue that can only victimise an entire people or an entire group. It is always 'They are all like that except …'

Except LaShawnqua, my good African American female neighbour, who is not like the rest of them. Except Dakota Black Horse, my Native Indian friend who is so hard-working and has nothing in common with, you know, other Indians. Except Abdelmalik, my Araboushim friend who abhors terrorism. Except Abdul Yahaya Jaiyeoba Okonkwo, my good Nigerian friend who is not into 419. Welcome to the world of the exception that is created, perhaps as a conscience-salving proposition, by the self and made to represent everything his people or group is not! The world of this exceptional creature is, however, a lonely one. Created by the self and perpetually hoisted as a trophy of exception, this character, who is not like his people or his group, is usually the entry point of a generalised process of denigration of the very people who sired him. He is the first victim of the very people who think they admire him by othering him!

This is Wole Soyinka's lonely and curious world in Igbo cyberdiscourse, raised to a cacophonous pitch recently by Soyinka's rightful disagreement with the cream of Yoruba leadership over their unbelievable and mischievous attempts to ethnicise the freedom action undertaken by the Movement for the Emancipation of the Niger Delta (MEND) against the Atlas Cove Jetty in Lagos – a property of Nigeria's oppressor-aggressor federal government. Soyinka's disagreement with certain voices in Yoruba leadership became an open sesame for so many Igbo voices on the Net – with a sprinkling of south-south voices – to manufacture him as 'the good Yoruba', thus tragically making Soyinka the latest addition to a long philosophico-historical list of othered and inferiorised subjects such as 'the good Indian', 'the good nigga', 'the good native', 'the good kaffir', and, of course, 'the good Muslim'.

Before they make another foolish post on this subject in Nigerian listservs, before they write another silly blog, before they make another uninformed chat-room comment, I will advise non-Yoruba who admire Soyinka by describing him as different from his people to urgently read Dorothy Hammond and Alta Jablow's *The Africa that Never Was: Four Centuries of British Writing about Africa*, Syed Hussein Alatas's *The Myth of the Lazy Native*, and Mahmood Mamdani's *Good Muslim, Bad Muslim* in order to gain some awareness of the historical and philosophical dimensions of the production of otherness. In *The Africa that Never Was*, our friends will discover how the bloody British spent four centuries manufacturing lazy and dishonest Africans – except the good African. In Alatas's book, they will discover how, in over three hundred years of contact, Western colonialists blanketed the Malays as lazy natives, a process in which they always systematically allowed just enough room for the 'one good Malay' who is not like the rest. In Mamdani's book, they will read how, in the aftermath of the 11 September terrorist attacks, it became the ideological strategy of a crusading Christian West, led by the crazy neocons around George Bush, to manufacture that good Muslim who, in the nature of things, is not like the terrorist rest! These are some of the introductory texts to my graduate seminar on the production of otherness.

One must make the concession that those non-Yoruba Internet voices who are hoisting Wole Soyinka as their trophy Yoruba genuinely believe that they admire and respect the man, being blissfully unaware of the insertion of their discourse into a broader frame of historical production of otherness, which ironically makes Soyinka the very first victim and target of their insults. Hence you encounter such silly comments as 'Soyinka is the only Yoruba with a truly nationalist outlook', 'Oh, how I wish other Yoruba people would emulate him', and other incrementally foolish and annoying statements in the same direction. One must also conclude that Soyinka's emergency admirers have simply never mentally self-projected into how they would feel if Nigerians from other ethnic groups suddenly began to hoist Chinua Achebe on a pole as the one good exception to his own people! To his own otherwise what people? Bad people? Useless people? And doing it in a most patronising and condescending manner to boot!

If there are folks who should be aware of the insulting nuances of otherness, it is precisely the Igbo Internet warriors who are now trafficking in Soyinka's otherness and so-called difference from his people. The Igbos have been such egregious targets and victims of this same process that it has become a near permanent feature of how they are represented on the Net by non-Igbo ethnicist jingoists. Every so often, you encounter foolish statements by so many non-Igbo emergency specialists of Igbo people and culture blanketing an entire people and culture with all the uncomplimentary epithets they can find in the dictionary. Such Nigerian racists would, of course, be quick to brandish the one Igbo friend they have or a previous sojourn in Igbo land as immunity against charges of being anti-Igbo.

This, in essence, is a terrain that those now trafficking in Soyinka's otherness and insulting him and his race in the process know only too well. And I wonder where they got the idea that Soyinka is a lone Yoruba voice in support of the agitations of the Niger Delta. By which abracadabra did they arrive at the conclusion that Soyinka is the only pan-Nigerian Yoruba nationalist? Where and when did they conduct their polling in Yoruba land? Just what is the empirical basis of their 'authoritative' submissions? Since most of those othering Soyinka as the only Yoruba avatar of Nigerian nationalism are in fact known Igbo irredentists, we must ask: Why would those who scream daily about the rebirth of the principles of Biafra – and whose sentiments one is fully sympathetic to – worry about anybody being a pan-Nigerian nationalist in the first place? What common ground could there possibly be between Igbo irredentism, rooted as it is in separatism, with the overload of pan-Nigerian nationalism? How and where do the two meet?

Quite frankly, with regard to MEND, Soyinka's voice pales beside that of Yinka Odumakin, human/civil/Yoruba rights activist and national publicity secretary of the Afenifere Renewal Group whose principled support for MEND and the spirit of the Niger Delta struggle is near legendary. Although it is not yet ascertained, the recent death threats Mr Odumakin received may not be totally unconnected with his support for MEND and the aspirations of the Niger Delta. The quiet hands of the nest of killers in Abuja may not be far from those threats. If this turns out to be true, what could possibly be more nationalistic than this Yoruba icon of the younger generation receiving threats to his life for his principled position on the Niger Delta question? Why is Odumakin not hoisted as the exception to his people? Ah, he has no Nobel! He is a less attractive candidate for otherness than a Nobel laureate. Soyinka is even far from being the most consistent Yoruba supporter of the legitimate agitations of the Niger Delta for equity, fairness, justice, and humane treatment within the Nigerian federation. He is just the most famous.

In fact, Soyinka has not been totally free of the occasional outrageous prevarication on the Niger Delta question. As recently as 2008, Soyinka advised the freedom fighters of the Niger Delta to lay down their arms and engage the federal government in what he called 'intellectual militancy'! I was alarmed and disappointed that such a hollow statement came from Soyinka at the time. What the heck is intellectual militancy? What, then, did Ken Saro-Wiwa do if not pacific intellectual militancy? And what was the response of the corrupt criminals running the federal government of Nigeria to Saro-Wiwa's intellectual militancy? How do you even begin to put anything intellectual and the charlatans of Abuja in the same bracket? Although one owes nobody any explanation, suffice it to state that I personally do not know any Yoruba in my own immediate intellectual and ideological spheres who isn't in full support of MEND and the spirit of the Niger Delta struggle.

I have yet to encounter anyone in my own networks and circuits of Yoruba intellectual like-minds who has any sympathy for the federal government of Nigeria. We are all unapologetically in support of the struggles of the peoples of the Niger Delta and all other Nigerian victims of the congenital criminals in Abuja. Have our friends even been reading Yoruba public intellectuals of my generation such as Professors Wale Adebanwi and Ebenezer Obadare? Those two friends of mine have been vocal and they are not unknown quantities in public discourse. Have they been reading Qansy Salako? As is, the Nigerian state is a criminal organisation in the hands of a cabal of deadly criminals in Abuja holding all of us hostage. From Umuechem to Agge, from Gbaramatu to Odi and Zaki Biam, the criminal actions of that state collectively dehumanise us, her victims. What, then, is so spectacular about Soyinka's principled call for a de-ethnicisation of the Atlas Cove freedom action that could possibly warrant the orgy of othering and insults that one has witnessed thus far?

I have stated time and again that those who invest in the production of otherness are often blind and deaf to the intrinsic humanism of their own cultures, starting with those odious Yoruba and Igbo characters who spend their lives exchanging unprintable and unhelpful rubbish about each other's ethnic groups online. They don't know how to read and listen to the great narratives of their own culture. What, for instance, does Chinua Achebe have to say about insulting anybody as the exception to his own people? Well, there is this guy called Ezeulu in *Arrow of God*. He tells the truth according to the ancestral protocols of his people: *My father told me that the land does not belong to us*. Just because Ezeulu's perception of the truth coincides with the white man's perception of things and goes against other versions of the truth by his people, Captain Winterbottom and other ignorant white men in the novel are quick to hoist him on a pole as 'the good Igbo' who is not like his people. The exception to his people! And because Ezeulu is somewhat light-skinned, the Europeans even surmise that he is able to tell the truth because there must have been a mix up in his bloodline – some light-skinned people must somehow have penetrated Ezeulu's pedigree along the way. The closer one is to whiteness, the better one is able to tell the truth. Of course!

What Winterbottom and the ignorant Europeans in *Arrow of God* do to Ezeulu is exactly what some of Soyinka's Igbo admirers online are doing to him! What part of *Arrow of God* have they not read? What on earth do they imagine Achebe is saying about the production of otherness? I am only waiting for them to surmise that there must have been a contamination of Soyinka's bloodline. Maybe some non-Yoruba blood was accidentally infused along the way? And they have already started on that path by seeking extraneous explanations outside of the Yoruba world for Soyinka's genius. One listserv commentator hinted and very nearly stated that Soyinka's genius devolves from his long history of association with Christopher Okigbo and Chinua Achebe. We just narrowly escaped claims that Okigbo and Achebe helped him write *Death and the King's Horseman*! Ever since I encountered that outrageous listserv comment, thankfully dismissed by the irrepressible Valentine Ojo, I have been wondering if my ability to string together a few sentences in English prose is not due to my brotherly association with Obi Nwakanma, Okey Ndibe, Chika Okeke-Agulu, Unoma Azuah, and so many other Igbo writers. You never know!

30

PAUL BIYA'S VACATION: AN IDEA FOR OBUDU CATTLE RANCH

'His country is one of the poorest and most corrupt in Africa but he sure can afford an expensive vacation. And the cost of his vacation is beginning to make tongues wag in La Baule.' That was how the news anchor of France 24 cable news station (France started that TV station in the vain hope of catching up with CNN and Al Jazeera) began her seven pm news broadcast on Wednesday, 3 September 2009. I hurriedly phoned to inform some Nigerian and French friends who were waiting for me at a pub around the Centre Georges Pompidou in Paris that I would be late. Something just cropped up on TV, bla bla bla. It was my last week in Paris and the friends had organised a beering session at the pub to bid me farewell. The following week, I would return to the grind of Canadian academia after two months in France.

Arriving late for my own send-off because of a news item on TV? That's the eternal damnation of the Nigerian/African in the West! Every time you hear 'Africa' or 'Nigeria' on TV, you behave like an antelope whose hypersensitive ears have just caught the tread of an unwelcome lion in the neighbourhood. I wasn't going to miss a France 24 news feature about the ongoing vacation of one of francophone Africa's most corrupt *Présidents à vie* (Presidents for life) and *Pères de la Nation* (Fathers of the Nation).

Details soon came with flamboyant footage of Monsieur le Président Biya holidaying with his wife in the French resort town of La Baule. As professional as she tried to be, the news anchor couldn't hide her disgust and contempt as she reeled out the details of how another African buffoon and his ostentatious wife 'are currently on an expensive holiday in La Baule'. Naturally, the Biyas have taken over the most expensive hotel in very expensive La Baule for their three-week vacation. They booked forty-three – yes, forty-three! – luxury rooms for themselves and aides! The price tag for the people of Cameroon? Only eight hundred thousand euros!

At this point, the focus shifts to the French journalist who started the investigation and blew the whistle on this crazy vacation. He gives the usual talking points that we hear regularly from Western liberal friends of Africa. He tells of how disgusting the whole thing is. He tells of what the money that the presidential couple has wasted could do for the starving children and women of Africa – yes, he said Africa, not Cameroon. I was about to scream in frustration at the Africanisation of the madness of the president of one specific African country when a better idea occurred to me ...

President and President Mrs Paul Biya have eight hundred thousand euros to blow on a three-week, forty-three-room vacation in France. You and I know that as African 'leaders', they will come again next year and even adjust their expenses for inflation. Since we can't stop them from coming, why don't we at least struggle to make them keep the money in the family back in Africa? Nigeria's Obudu Cattle Ranch in Cross

River state is walking distance from the Biyas. I suggest that the management of Obudu, the governor of Cross River state, and the minister of tourism send a high-powered delegation to Yaoundé with immediate effect to offer a discounted summer vacation at Obudu to the presidential couple of Cameroon. Eight hundred thousand euros is a lot of money and we could use it in Nigeria. Do they really need it in France? If we know how to market the tourism potential of Obudu properly, we just might be able to convince the Biyas to bring that excess Cameroonian money to Nigeria next year. After all, it could even be Nigerian money that they are spending in France! There is no telling whether Cameroon has already started making money from the oil reserves in the Bakassi peninsula, hence the very expensive holiday in La Baule.

Back to the news. The mayor of La Baule was interviewed for the clip. He showered praises on the presidential couple and commented on the friendship between the people of La Baule and the people of Cameroon! Asked if he was aware of the fact that the Biyas' vacation in his town contributes to corruption in Africa, he smiled and quipped, 'No comments.' My friends at the pub had comments when I finally joined them. I announced my intention to write and publish this piece in the Nigerian newspaper *NEXT*. 'You would be doing the Nigerian people a disservice.' one of them said. I replied, 'You don start again o. Wetin be disservice for inside dis matter?' My friend responded: 'If you write and publish that President Biya spent eight hundred thousand euros on forty-three hotel rooms in Europe, don't be surprised to hear next year that a Nigerian governor, senator, or rep has spent two million euros on seventy rooms in La Baule. You will just give the looters of Abuja ideas on where next to spend their loot.' I kept quiet. There is nothing a group of Nigerians can't say over beer when discussing our disgraceful rulers. How do you respond to that one?

31

WHY I WILL
NOT EMULATE JESUS

Once again, Easter came with the usual greetings and exhortations from the rulers of Nigeria. Religious holidays always provide an occasion for the Nigerian ruling class to issue robotic and wooden exhortations asking the people to emulate the exemplary lives of Jesus or Muhammad. I've had to deal with such exhortations my entire life. This year, I have decided not to listen to President Yar'Adua and the thirty-six state governors. Let them sell their exhortations to the marines. I have no intention of emulating Jesus this time around. Rather, I prefer to don my thinking cap and ask why I am always urged to emulate Jesus or Muhammad by rulers whose lifestyles and (mis)handling of our affairs are diametrically opposed to the prescriptions of both deities. Why are President Yar'Adua and the state governors so anxious to have me emulate Jesus?

The more I think about it, the more it appears odd that we are not being asked to emulate the Nigerian sons of Jesus, who, after all, are closer to the corridors of power in Abuja and the state capitals than Jesus and Muhammad combined. Why, for instance, would President Yar'Adua not ask me to emulate Chris Oyakhilome, one of Jesus' more prominent Nigerian sons? Perhaps the president read it in my stars that I am allergic to Pastor Chris's Savile Row suits? Or maybe someone told him that I wouldn't look cool in Pastor Kris Okotie's Ferragamo shoes and designer watches? I don't even mind emulating Pastor Okotie's Jheri curls but I am growing bald. And how about trying to emulate travelling in style in private jets like Pastors Enoch Adeboye and David Oyedepo? Again, why would Abuja want me to emulate Jesus and not his abundantly blessed Nigerian sons? In African culture, fathers pray for their sons to fare much better than them in life, materially. That prayer has worked for the Nigerian sons of Jesus. Shouldn't the prayer continue its logical progression by making sure that we, the grandsons, are even more materially successful than the pastors listed above?

I think I know why the rulers of Nigeria want to turn back the hands of the material clock by making us all look like Jesus and not his contemporary Nigerian sons. A good number of Nigerians already enjoy the standard of living Jesus had two thousand years ago, and some even live below what Jesus would have considered the poverty level of his time, manger, warts and all. By constantly asking us to emulate him, the rulers of Nigeria are indirectly expressing their interest in the maintenance of the status quo. Consider transportation. Jesus covered extraordinary mileage on foot. The only time he got a ride was when he 'chanced' somebody and conscripted a donkey for the triumphal entry into Jerusalem. So severe was the recession at the time that he couldn't even afford to buy the donkey. And he was content to enter Jerusalem in a *keteketecade* and not a motorcade like the rulers of Nigeria. Imagine the problems we would solve for President Yar'Adua if we all agreed to emulate the transportation tastes of Jesus literally. He wouldn't have to suffer the indignity of being asked to perform and rejig our corrupt and comatose petroleum industry. No more exportation of crude for reimportation for domestic use. We would all be riding donkeys. That would also boost the economy of his home state of Katsina since all the donkeys would come from northern Nigeria.

People have been complaining about an impending food doom. The predictions coming from the international community, the World Bank, Oxfam, Madonna, Bono, and Jeffrey Sachs are simply alarming. Everyone is predicting massive food shortages for Africa in the near future. Nigeria is already having to import rice, beans, and virtually everything else we eat. A good friend of mine here in Ottawa, Mazi Ebere, used to joke that Nigeria would soon import *elubo* and *efo riro* from China. Today, Mazi Ebere would be the first to confess that this is now a real possibility and no longer a joke. We all know that Jesus was constantly fasting. He once fasted for forty days and forty nights. Not even the brilliant Lucifer could tempt him to grab a bite with all the incentives in this world. Imagine the weight that would be lifted off President Yar'Adua's shoulders if 150 million Nigerians decided to emulate the dietary practices of Jesus by fasting all the time, especially during the forty days and forty nights preceding the presidential elections of 2011! Imagine if we all refused to eat even if President Yar'Adua bribed us with miracles such as regular electricity and respite from armed robbery! No more rice importation. No more worrying about performing in the agricultural sector. Certainly, getting us to emulate Jesus is President Yar'Adua's surest path to a second term in office! That is why I will not emulate Jesus at all.

ENDNOTES

1   I subsequently never made it to the major seminary after high school.

2   A dog is always sacrificed during Ogun festival. The neck is severed in one blow of the machete. Apprehension of Ogun festival is always a source of culture clash for Westerners who come with a different attitude to dogs.

3   Enoch Adeboye is the General Overseer of the Redeemed Christian Church of God, Nigeria's most populous Pentecostal church and part of the new wave of prosperity Pentecostalism.

4   For nearly three decades (1960s-1980s), the Catholic church in central and eastern Nigeria was home to many Québecois missionary priests of the Spiritan priestly order.

5   The highway links Lagos, Nigeria's commercial capital, with Ibadan, West Africa's largest city. Land bordering the highway has been taken over by Pentecostal churches and this often causes mega traffic jams.

6   In 1986, General Ibrahim Babangida, the despot ruling Nigeria at the time, yielded to pressure from the IMF and the World Bank and introduced the Structural Adjustment Programme (SAP). This led to hyper-inflation and destroyed the country's vibrant middle class. Food and everyday groceries became unaffordable. Government reacted by distributing subsidised rice, beans, vegetable oil, laundry detergent etc. to government workers. Goverment called those 'essential commodities'. Nigerians shortened it to 'essenco'.

7   A respected Nigerian public intellectual and fiery social critic who died in the 1980s.

8   A famous economist who left academia for the murky waters of Nigerian politics after a spell as governor of the country's central bank.

9   Aso Rock Villa is the seat of Nigeria's federal government in the capital city of Abuja.

10   The Peoples Democratic Party is the ruling party in Nigeria. It
      has been in power since the country's return to democracy in
      1999.

11   See his book of the same title.

12   See Wole Soyinka's account of this trip in his widely-circulated
      essay, 'The Isle of Polyphemus' (http://www.usafricaonline
      .com/palestine.soyinka.html). See also Breyten Breytenbach's
      account in his essay, 'An Open Letter to General Ariel Sharon'
      (http://www.thenation.com/article/open-letter-general
      -ariel-sharon).

13   http://news.biafranigeriaworld.com/archive/ngguardian
      /2002/dec/04/article08.html

14   Nigeria's ruling elite love to think of Nigeria as the giant of
      Africa.

15   Ghana's president at the time.

16   http://www.whirledbank.org/ourwords/summers.html